Tarts Anon

Sweet and savoury
tart brilliance

Hardie Grant

BOOKS

Gareth Whitton, co-authored with Catherine Way

Contents

The Tarts

The Trim

Introduction

Foreword

by Melissa Leong

> From a rustic quiche to a wobbly,
> nutmeg-spiked custard, or an acute
> angle of jewel-bright sharp lemon tang,
> I've rarely met a tart I didn't like.
> And neither, I suspect, have you.

To me, tarts occupy a worthy place in the pantheon of pastry because a properly good one manages to deceive us with doe-eyed innocence, while delivering an unexpected punch in the face when it comes to flavour, texture and aroma. A heaping dose of nostalgia doesn't go astray, either. An open pastry shell occupied by a sweet or savoury filling, but beyond that, the world's your oyster. With so many possibilities, what sets a transcendental tart apart from a middle-of-the-road one is the detail.

The birth of Tarts Anon is the story of what can go right, even in the wrong conditions. Forged in the fires of a post high-profile pastry position, pandemic-related life (try saying that thrice), Gareth's lockdown baking and Cat's entrepreneurial powers combined to produce a gift for dessert tragics of Melbourne: tarts made with utter precision. Sharp little slices of punchy flavour and sublime texture. Satisfyingly sharp wedges of goodness, art in form alone. A study in realising that an effortless end result requires significant skill.

From classic to modern, their menu inspiration took us around the globe at a time when we couldn't take ourselves. An Italian-inspired tiramisu tart, a journey to the tropical climes of Malaysia for lush coconut and pandan vibes, a very British-inspired Earl Grey, chocolate and caraway nod to Heston Blumenthal, and a pumpkin spiced caramel tart from the United States (naturally). All of it rooted in the foundations of classical French pastry techniques. In a time where little made sense in the world, tarts became a life raft of purpose for Gareth; a resounding answer to 'what next?' when it came to career.

What he didn't see coming next was that by saying yes to the insanity of reality television, tarts would lead Gareth to become *MasterChef*'s very first Dessert Master. To compete among other professional pastry peers – and win – required more than just skill, tenacity, and technique (they all have that). More even, than a distinct pastry identity (they all have that, too). Gareth's winning combo turned out to be a little luck, a lot of hard-earned experience during the heat of service, and the ability to hit his straps when it counts (late bloomers and those who find themselves lost at times, take note).

As the author of a foreword, I'm supposed to give you a bunch of reasons why you should buy, read and cook from this book. That part's easy: this book is a succinct, approachable collection of well-honed tips, tricks, techniques and pieces of advice on tart making. It also contains base recipes, sub recipes and essential equipment sure to amp up damn near anyone's tart game, no matter who you are.

With a great tart, the devil is in the detail. And all the detail you're likely to need can be found between these covers, whether you're a keen home baker, or beyond.

Why Tarts?

An Introduction by Gareth Whitton

> Over and over, we've been asked,
> 'Why tarts?' It's a good question.
>
> It was never meant to be tarts.

I lost my job as head pastry chef at Dinner by Heston Blumenthal Melbourne when the restaurant closed down in early 2020 – and promptly slid into an early-onset midlife crisis. After years of long nights and anti-social rosters, I reasoned it was the perfect time to throw in the towel with hospitality. I applied for account manager positions in the food sector, recruitment jobs, and I even entertained the idea of going to university. Then in March, when the realities of COVID-19 set in, I was still unemployed. Eventually, I found myself applying for anything that was going, which turned out to be a job at a supermarket. There's nothing like being well outside of your comfort zone to make you realise you how good you had it.

I'd never truly thought of myself as a pastry chef, a feeling that had always been reinforced by my colleagues. Too much of a chef for pastry town, too much of a pastry chef for the kitchen. And, although I'd spent most of the last few years of my career in pastry, I always wanted to stay in touch with the other side – to be a 'jack of all trades', if you will. As a result, I'd never really plumbed the depths of pastry and pastry making, working solely in restaurants and never in a bakery or boulangerie.

But over the months that I restocked and organised confectionery and cat soup (literally soup for cats) on supermarket shelves, I found myself coming around to the fact that the kitchen was where I belonged.

Meanwhile, my partner Catherine had suggested we do some baking at home as a 'fun' lockdown activity. I didn't immediately acquiesce. At that stage of lockdown I had already found a fairly stable weekend routine of riding my bike much longer than the one hour of exercise and 5 km (3 mile) limit allowed, then settling in for a long afternoon of drinking red wine and watching TV on the couch. Catherine was persistent, however, and sure enough doing some baking at home was enough to get my creative juices flowing again. I started playing around with a few different techniques and recipes, but tarts became the go-to.

Tarts have always been quite special to me. This started with making a plum and almond tart in my first kitchen job in my hometown in the Southern Highlands of New South Wales. It carried on later in my career to whenever it was my turn to make staff dessert. I'd smash out a tart and fill it with whatever fruit or chocolate trim was taking up real estate on the staff shelf. That tiny bit of extra effort to make a pastry base to fill with the kitchen scraps that usually found their way to the staff table was enough to make the rest of the team think that they had been treated to something special (possibly with the exception of the huge failure that was a white asparagus and white chocolate ganache tart that I once made – a recipe you will not find in the pages of this book). And yet, when I arrived at Dinner by Heston in London, despite public expectations of fireworks, liquid nitrogen, and culinary deception at every turn, I was somewhat taken aback to see a plain custard tart on the menu. In time, I understood that this was the very essence of Heston's food – it was classic, consistent, delicious and unique enough to make it stand out in its own way. Every element in every dish had a purpose and every recipe was tried and tested to be the best version of itself.

This was the ethos I brought into Tarts Anon. Through many trials, we established a good little business model that did exactly what it said on the box. We did one thing, and we did it well (or, as well as we could with what we had at our disposal, which was a domestic oven, a rolling pin and mostly home brand ingredients). It was the side-hustle-est of all side hustles, baking tarts on the weekends in and amongst our two full time jobs.

I was always willing to abandon the lockdown project at the drop of a hat and regain focus on my career. As the months ticked on, I'd swapped stacking shelves for working at Lune Croissanterie – a workplace which became a huge inspiration for the eventual direction of Tarts Anon – with its technically superb creations that would emerge from the oven requiring little more than a dusting of this or that to reach their complete, perfect form. My inclination to keep Tarts Anon small and not give it the validation that it deserved was strong. We moved house to a bigger kitchen and a bigger oven, anything to keep the business at home. As time went on, however, tarts were increasingly at the forefront of my mind. It was hard not to keep wanting to make more and more tarts each weekend when the demand was so high. Eventually I succumbed to the pressure (the local council were onto us) and we signed a lease for a co-working kitchen space in Collingwood. The idea that Tarts Anon would only be a lockdown project was growing weaker by the day.

People around me saw Tarts Anon's potential far before I did. Catherine was rallying friends and family to convince me to put more effort into expanding the business; even my bosses at Lune Croissanterie saw promise in my side hustle. I started to see the faint outline of a full-time job as a business owner appear.

So, why tarts? Perhaps the real answer is that my whole career to this point has been leading up to what we now call Tarts Anon. We just had to add a global pandemic, an existential pastry crisis and dodgy microwave-oven to get the recipe just right.

The Makings of Tarts Anon

An Introduction by Catherine Way

We went through the stages of Melbourne's pandemic lockdown not too dissimilarly to many (then) childless couples in their thirties. Puzzles, day drinking, indoor fitness and a newfound love for walking. We applied to adopt a rescue puppy, learnt a dance to a trending song, and did the Sunday quiz over Zoom – all pretty cookie-cutter stuff.

But as we trudged into the depths of winter, I convinced Gareth that we could bake together on weekends as an activity. For full disclosure, I have no baking skills whatsoever, and, in hindsight, I had little interest in learning. Really, I was trying to manufacture one of those stereotypical movie scenes where we'd throw flour on each other's faces and giggle, as he held the bowl and I stirred the wooden spoon.

Turns out I had completely underestimated Gareth's need for control in the kitchen and his no-nonsense attitude towards baking. 'Wait, why are you doing that?' 'Here, do it like this.' 'Are you actually cutting those peaches with a serrated knife?' (I was). Gareth simply couldn't follow the recipe I'd chosen, a tart from *Beatrix Bakes* ('I have an idea!') and he certainly couldn't let my substandard pastry techniques and fantasy of a romantic afternoon get in the way of pastry precision. Soon enough, I had doffed my apron and taken out my digital camera to photograph the process with not even a fleck of flour on my face.

But as Gareth continued to return to baking (unforced) come weekends, I was mesmerised by the utter precision of the tarts that he managed to create in our hybrid microwave-oven (which had a tendency to malfunction and switch between the two settings while baking).

I wondered if we could sell the tarts on weekends to earn us some extra income. I enjoyed photography and knew my way around Instagram, I reasoned in my head – but the catch was that Gareth, being the pastry chef, would have to do most of the work. I broached the idea with him one morning. He literally groaned.

Months went by before I was able to convince Gareth to allow me to drop some flyers in our neighbour's letterboxes in an attempt to sell the tarts. 'People are bored,' I insisted. 'These tarts are delicious,' I gassed. 'It'll be fun,' I nagged. Gareth's initial resistance was, for me, to be expected. However, after eight years of dating, I also knew that he'd eventually succumb to my will. In fact, I had already set up an Instagram page with a logo and images aggressively captioned 'COMING SOON.' While I waited for a virtual meeting to start, I made a post in our local neighbourhood Facebook page. The response was beyond believable and soon Gareth was baking ten tarts every weekend from home, then twenty. I had to introduce a rule that people couldn't order two weekends in a row. I stopped people from ordering more than one whole tart and told people who wanted a half that there was only a quarter left so we could serve as many people as possible week to week. It was never enough, though, and the fervour was real. For the next year, there wasn't a single week that Gareth's tarts didn't sell out. He was so in denial about the whole thing that he didn't even try to negotiate on the name of the business, which, admittedly, we both now hate.

With a commercial kitchen and more fridges, Gareth could streamline his baking and pump out seventy tarts per week. It still wasn't enough. I got tendonitis from sending too many DMs. Gareth was burnt out from working at Lune Croissanterie and baking for Tarts Anon on the weekends. In September 2021, the opportunity came up to move into our own kitchen and open a shopfront, and we decided to take the plunge. The rent was affordable and Gareth was probably too tired to object.

Tarts Anon had found a home.

Our Tart Making Ethos

Tarts are, in our opinion, the perfect dessert. They are the one pastry form that is able to transcend all genres, from top-end dining to regional bakeries.

At a minimum, you get buttery, melt-in-your-mouth pastry, which is in turn a vessel for an unlimited array of flavours and textures. Then there's the beauty of taking something so entrenched in history and bringing it into the twenty-first century with modern techniques. This is not a new concept by any means, but is something that inspires Gareth as a chef.

Once a tart comes out of the oven, there is minimal interference with the product lest the integrity be lost. It's all in the technique. Not garnishing techniques, or plating techniques, but solid fundamental pastry techniques that dictate how the tart will taste and look without any finishing touches. Something that would just come out of the oven complete, its aesthetic left in the hands of the elements. We've never gone down the path of building desserts inside tarts shells, or adorning with fruits and tuiles. And to this day, with a few notable exceptions, this is something that we have not only refused to employ, but has never tempted us. Sure, the finishing touches may have become more complex than dustings of icing sugar or cocoa powder – carpets of chives or velvety coatings of pectin-set glazes have joined the repertoire now, but the philosophy remains the same.

But for all our focus on technique, our tarts are not really designed to be thought provoking or 'educational' like some dishes that have come out of restaurants Gareth cut his teeth in. They're designed to be relatable. Although the odd one comes up that is completely original, for the most part flavour combos the world over have almost all been done; the good ones anyway. So we accept this – knowing full well that the best way we can be creative here is to help our customers revisit old memories, or surprise them with something that they thought they knew. We have tried to set ourselves apart by ensuring that everything we want to include in the tart would be part of its composition. If it couldn't be worked into the body of the tart, it would usually be back to the drawing board.

Our process of flavour building revolves around how you eat it. Given the shape of a tart slice, the most logical way to eat it is point to crust, pizza style. We imagine most people are getting a mouthful of the cross section, so we want that mouthful to involve every layer, and experience the same texture and flavour profile all the way through.

To achieve a balanced mouthful, we employ something called flavour encapsulation. This means that instead of diluting the intensity of a certain flavour and increasing its volume, we add intensified and concentrated elements in a certain area of the tart, so that when it is eaten, then its flavour disperses evenly through the other elements, providing the balance.

A good example of this is the Passionfruit and Ginger Tart (page 124). The custard itself could have lovely, subtle undertones of ginger through it, and the jam could be a perfumed passionfruit jam with a suggestion of spicy ginger notes. What we've done instead is made a offensively strong ginger jam that when eaten alone could summon the dead. But, underneath a refreshingly tropical passionfruit custard, it strikes the perfect balance.

This all said, our approach to tart making doesn't mean we don't think the tarts you get at the local bakery aren't also bloody incredible. I mean, it's butter and sugar, right? But if you take the refinement of fine-dining cooking and the familiarity of your local bakery, then you have an idea of what we're aspiring to. Capturing what makes a tart exceptional and being able to serve that same thing in a pizza box is a fine line of high–low balance we try to tread seamlessly.

Moving into a shared commercial kitchen space and then to our own kitchen, hiring staff and using quality suppliers has meant the benchmark for what we consider doing something 'well' has increased immeasurably. With the equipment, staff and space to push every element in every tart to its 'best version', doing something 'well' became more of an understatement. In fact, we're striving to do it brilliantly – and it's this desire to innovate that keeps us going.

How to Use This Book

It may seem self-evident, but tarts are no piece of cake. And although the scale of what we do has changed since we moved into a commercial kitchen, remember this was once a home project too.

This cookbook is the culmination of all the techniques and tips we have tirelessly refined since starting Tarts Anon – and in technique we trust. We hope you find this without pretence, the same way we wish to serve our tarts. We want you to create tarts that we would want to eat ourselves, every day of the week and for every occasion.

All the foundational techniques are explained in detail here at the beginning of the book. In the first chapter, 'Classic Tarts', you'll find the tarts we think are the perfect building blocks to master before tackling some of the more challenging recipes in the following chapters. It includes the recipes for the very first tarts that we made in our home kitchen, including some that are, to this day, our most popular creations.

As you move through the book, you'll also notice that many of the processes that we use for making custards, jams and frangipanes use similar techniques. This is intentional, we are not trying to reinvent the wheel with each recipe, but simply make a tart that is undeniably the best version of itself.

Each tart will require a preprepared shortcrust pastry shell, which is the very first recipe. Some tarts will require one more bake to set a custard filling, some even two more bakes. Loosely, our tarts can be divided into the categories of: 'custard based tarts', 'cake tarts' and 'hybrid tarts' (cake tarts with a custard layer).

When you make a batch of dough, you could make a double or triple batch and freeze this to use in future bakes, which will save you some time as all our recipes use this same dough recipe.

Please pay attention to the 'tips and tricks' we offer throughout the book (we have compiled these through both a near lifetime of working in professional kitchens and some, at times, devastating failures in our own baking escapades). A word of warning, do NOT start any baking until you have flipped through to page 136 and become one of the most loyal patients of dulce de leche, aka Dr Dulce. Trust us – he bulk bills. And if Dr Dulce can't ease your tarty ills, then we've included a 'Quick Troubleshooting Guide' (page 197) to use as a reference point. But remember, imperfections in your tarts will most certainly ensure an improvement in your next bake so, keep on rolling (we couldn't resist)!

Our recipes have been put together with a lot of consideration. Where possible, we have thrown in suggested swaps, but there are also some that just won't yield the same results if tweaked. If there is something you're not able to get your hands on, then in many cases, that recipe just won't be achievable. We have made a concerted effort to make sure these recipes are achievable in the home kitchen, but on occasion, a particular setting agent or a hand-held blender are absolute musts. Likewise, some of the recipes for the components in the tarts will yield slightly more than you will need for one individual tart. Excess wastage isn't ideal but we'd rather you make slightly more of a perfect glaze or caramel, versus the perfect amount of an inferior product.

Finally, you won't find dustings of gold leaf (okay, once) or pastry tuilles, etc. for covering up mistakes because we believe if you can get the building blocks right, the rest should be, as they say, a piece of cake.

A note on oven temperatures and measurements:
Oven temperatures in this book are for fan-forced ovens. If you're using a conventional oven, increase the temperature by 20°C (70°F).

Measurements are generally given by weight to ensure consistency. You'll notice that assembly instructions will often require you to weigh out the components. This is to ensure consistency across your bakes.

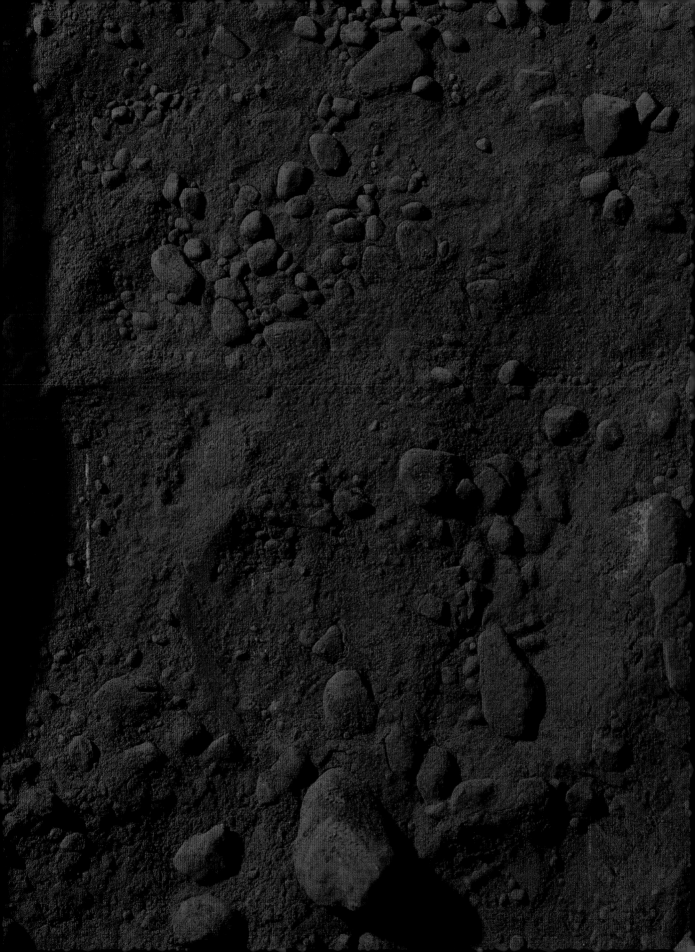

Key Ingredients

Flour
Use all-purpose (plain) flour or cake flour for all the recipes unless stated otherwise. Low protein flours such as these (as opposed to 00 or T55 flours, which are higher in protein) help to slow gluten activation within the flour, resulting in a light, fluffy cake and crisp, short pastry.

Butter
Use unsalted butter for these recipes unless stated otherwise. In our kitchen we use Pepe Saya butter, which we find to be the most consistent and delicious (and can be sourced readily in Australia).

Cream
Most of the recipes will either call for pouring cream or double cream, or sometimes both. Double cream is used in recipes that feature custards, where an increased fat percentage is required to enable your mix to set once cooked. As such, they're not interchangeable! For pouring cream, use a minimum of 30–35% fat. Double cream has a fat percentage of 45% or more.

Sugar
We use lots of different sugars. The type of sugar you use will set the foundation for the flavour profile of your recipe. For example, we tend to use the least refined (brown sugar, golden syrup, etc.) for tarts with darker, warmer and more caramelly vibes and leave white sugars for the lighter and fruitier preparations.

Chocolate
Most supermarket chocolates are fine, but make sure you're only using couverture chocolate in these recipes. We prefer to use callets and buttons because they melt more evenly, however you can achieve a similar result by chopping a block of chocolate into small pieces before melting.

Condensed milk
Woolworths Homebrand is the only one we will ever use, unless we are literally without any other option. Please don't sell them out. If you are unable to source this one, any brand will do the same job, however it is worth playing around with the brands available to you to find one that will come out of the can once cooked as firm as possible.

Pectin (and its variants)
Interestingly, the majority of the world's pectins are made in the same place, so you won't find many differences between the different brands. Certain pectins used in these recipes can be tricky to find. You will need to buy them online or at specialty pastry shops (e.g. Savour, Simon Johnson). The pectins you readily find at the supermarket (e.g. Jamsetta) have added sugars and acidity regulators and therefore will not work in the glazing recipes.

Cheese
For the love of god, please use good quality cheese!

A note on dietaries
Our business leans heavily on gluten and dairy. We receive multiple requests for gluten free or vegan products in the shop each week, and while we'd love to cater to these requests (and take your money), unfortunately gluten-free pastry or swapping vegan alternatives for the fundamental ingredients in our recipes could make that particular tart possibly still delicious, but unlikely as delicious as the rest of the menu. That said, it's very likely that you'll be able to find a great gluten-free pastry recipe to use instead of our recipe and fill it with many of the recipes in this book that don't contain gluten.

Key Equipment

Tart tin
25 × 3.5 cm (approx. 10 × 1½ in) fluted tart tin with a removable base. This is our standard size of tart tin and is required for your tarts to come out the same way. You can purchase these online or from a kitchen supply store.

Rolling pin
Preferably one without handles on the ends.

Baking paper
Silicone-coated greaseproof paper. Note: you get what you pay for with cheaper brands.

Aluminium Foil
Try to get yourself some that is 40 cm (approx. 15¾ in) wide. This will make lining pastry shells that little bit easier, as you will be able to use a single piece.

Microplane
Useful for shaving down the edges of the pastry shell once baked for a smooth, straight edge. Also necessary for finely grating finishing touches over the tarts.

Mandolin
Use for thinly slicing fruit and vegetables. Also, make sure you pretend to cut your finger off each time you use it for a hilarious gag (but don't actually cut your finger off, as this is decidedly less hilarious.).

Sieves
We use four different types of sieves at the shop. The finer ones are for passing (e.g. custard mixes and caramels); the coarser ones are for dusting (e.g. icing/confectioners' sugar or cocoa) on top of your tarts. You can get away with just one good one.

Thermometer
A digital one is key for accurately measuring the temperature of the caramels and jams.

Maryse spatula
These flat, flexible spatulas are necessary for removing all the contents from your mixing bowl (so your recipe remains accurate) and for stirring custard mixes. We suggest you invest in one!

Hand-held blender
You will need this for most recipes. It's imperative for creating emulsions (such as custard and caramel mixes) and integral if you plan on making any of the tarts that have dairy-based glazes.

Knives
Sharp knives are critical for precision cuts and portioning. You'll need a paring knife, a good bread knife and a large chef's knife. And the sharper the better, in all cases.

Heat-proof bowls
You'll need these to melt chocolate and for working with hot mixtures.

Measuring jugs
But not for measuring (this is what a scale is for). You will need these to pour your custards into the pastry shells. A smaller, narrow jug will come in handy for when you need to blend your glazes.

A good set of scales
Digital, please. As a wise man once said, 'Speak to me in grams or portions.'

Plastic scraper
The great, multi-purpose kitchen tool.

Whisk
Gareth is a man of many whisks, but you will need at least one approx. 20 cm (8 in) balloon whisk.

Saucepans, pots, frying pans
Yep, you'll need 'em.

The (not so) Basics

Our Pastry Recipe

Our pastry, in its essence, is what makes Tarts Anon *Tarts Anon*. It's a showcase of technique and does take practice (and patience) to master.

All of our tarts, sweet and savoury, use the same pastry recipe. In fact, it's the same recipe we've been using since day one (although the method has changed slightly to accommodate larger and larger batches).

Traditional pâte brisée is a lot 'shorter' than our recipe. The name itself (which translates to 'broken pastry') suggests that it should crumble and dissolve in the mouth, and as wonderful as this is to eat in a controlled environment, it isn't very receptive to being placed in a box and being driven halfway across Melbourne in the passenger foot space of your car (note: we don't recommend this transportation method). So to get the texture, robustness and flavour that we require, we removed enough butter to create a biscuity texture that is still delicious in its own right, but that can still be picked up and eaten 'hand-pie' style by the most discerning of tart fans (ourselves included).

The process for making our pastry in the shop takes three days, but for the book we've put together an abridged version. We figured that after three days you'd almost certainly be planning to sneak a slice under the light of the fridge door, away from the judging eyes of your loved ones, not gearing yourself up for phase two of making pastry. Also, as we discuss in the next section, this much resting is unnecessary for smaller batches of dough. This version will be just as successful and delicious. We recommend nailing it, because it will form the basis for all of the following recipes.

Shortcrust Pastry (Pâte Brisée)
Makes 1 tart shell

200 g (7 oz) plain (all-purpose) flour
100 g (3½ oz) cold unsalted butter, cut into cubes
3 g (0.1 oz) salt
50 g (1¾ oz) water

The Process

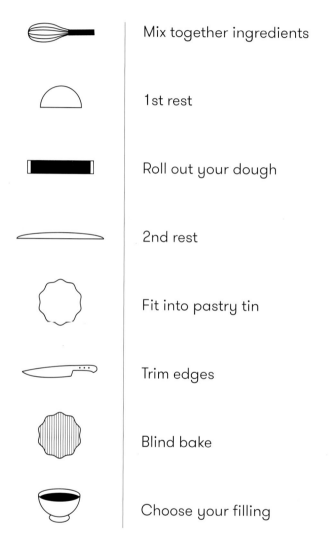

Mix together ingredients

1st rest

Roll out your dough

2nd rest

Fit into pastry tin

Trim edges

Blind bake

Choose your filling

1   Place the butter, flour and salt into a bowl
    (this process can also be done in a kitchen stand
    mixer or food processor). Using your fingers, work
    the ingredients together until they resemble fine
    bread crumbs and no lumps of butter are present.

2   Add the water a little at a time (or in a steady
    stream if using a kitchen stand mixer), until
    it forms a firm but malleable mixture. If you
    used a food processor earlier, it'd be best to
    finish this one off by hand.

3   Move the dough to your benchtop and work
    into a puck-sized shape. Wrap with plastic
    wrap and allow to rest in the fridge for at
    least 30 minutes.

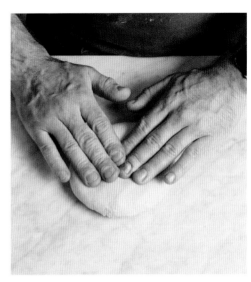

4   Preheat your oven to 180°C (360°F). Place the
     pastry on a piece of baking paper and cover with
     a second piece of baking paper. Using a rolling
     pin, roll out the pastry into a circle roughly 35 cm
     (approx. 13¾ in) wide, and around 3 mm (⅛ in)
     thick. Allow the pastry to firm up again in the
     fridge for at least an hour before lining the tin
     (if lining the tin immediately, be sure to rest it for
     at least an hour).

5   Remove one piece of baking paper from the pastry
     and drape the pastry over your tart tin. You may
     find this easier to do by using a rolling pin.

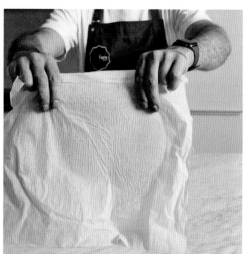

6   Press the pastry into the knuckles of the tart
     tin using the flats of your fingers.

7   Use a sharp knife to remove any excess trim from the edges of the pastry. Allow the pastry to sit for 15 minutes or so in the freezer for one final rest.

8   Take one large sheet of aluminium foil and gently press into the edges of the pastry shell, ensuring that the sheet is big enough to go over the edge and completely line the tart. Fill it to the brim with uncooked rice, then fold the foil gently back over the top and place into the oven.

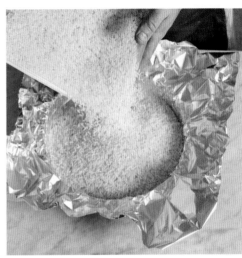

9   Bake for 25–30 minutes, or until the edges of the pastry are a nice medium-golden colour. Remove from the oven and sneak a look under the foil to check the doneness. Cook until the colour is consistent, then allow to cool at room temperature. Remove the foil and rice when cool enough to touch.

In a Little More Detail

Consider the following pages your extra credit reading on pastry making. We've broken down the five major steps – mixing, resting, rolling, lining and baking – in a little more detail.

Mixing

We mix our pastry together using a 'crumbing method', which ensures a crispy-yet-tender result and prevents the pastry shell from shrinking in the oven.

It works like this: By mixing cold butter into flour, the butter remains cold as it mixes and can break up into smaller pieces that coat each granule of flour with a layer of solidified fat. Ideally, the mixture will resemble almond meal when you finish mixing it. This crumbing method encourages the creation of air pockets that become trapped in the pastry as the fat melts away, which will make the pastry tender and crisp.

If you were to use liquid fat, such as oil or melted butter, it would absorb into the flour particles and make it impossible to establish bonds between the gluten proteins present in the flour, causing your pastry to become excessively crumbly and impossible to handle. If the ingredients aren't cold – say if the pieces of butter haven't been cut small enough to begin

with, or if you handle your dough too much and warm it up – then you run the risk of this happening before each flour granule has had the opportunity to protect itself from the moisture with its fatty barrier. (If you're baking in a warm room, you could refrigerate your flour to make sure both the flour and butter remain cold enough to avoid this situation.) This also tends to make the dough shrink in the oven, as no gluten network has formed, and the fat just melts away as it heats.

When making this type of pastry, we are looking to establish connections between gluten proteins, but not strengthen them. This means that the pastry will be robust enough to hold its shape, but still be delicate enough to crumble when eaten.

For water to eventually absorb into the flour and create this gluten structure, the temperature of the butter and the size of the pieces are key. The size impacts the speed at which the fats in the butter liquify, and subsequently absorb into the flour particles.

It's important to remember that gluten strands will form in your dough while you are working it, so the goal is to mix the dough only to the point where it just comes together. The more you work your dough, the more gluten strands will form, leading to a tough dough that will shrink in the oven.

Water is essential to the formation of the gluten structure, and this structure is critical – particularly in our recipe. Not only does it make the dough able to be handled at every stage of the pastry-making process, but it also allows for the creation of texture in the pastry. The pastry is hydrated by adding, well, water, but also with butter. Most butters sit at around 15% water content, so it is perfect for creating the desired texture for our pastry without compromising on flavour as you would with other solid fats such as vegetable shortening or lard (which are closer to 100% fat). The important takeaway here is that the less water your butter contains, the crispier your pastry will be.

Another critical consideration in mixing is the equipment you use. When making pastry for one tart shell, you'll be able to get away with making the pastry by hand. You should be able to work by hand when making up to five or six batches, but after that it gets tricky. Getting enough friction through the mixture to properly distribute the flour requires a lot of hard work, which only increases the larger the batches become. With this hard work comes increased time, which in turn will start to generate the problems with the strengthening of gluten structures mentioned earlier. To make larger batches of dough, you'll need to introduce some level of assistance, such as a kitchen stand mixer. This will not only speed up the process, but also make your results more consistent.

Resting

As the dough sits, the water molecules will hydrate the flour particles. During this time, the bonds that were formed between the gluten proteins during mixing will have a chance to relax. This is critical as any tension that was created in these bonds from the mixing process will retract when exposed to heat, resulting in shrinkage and cracking. Creating tension is unavoidable during the mixing stage, so the resting stage is essential.

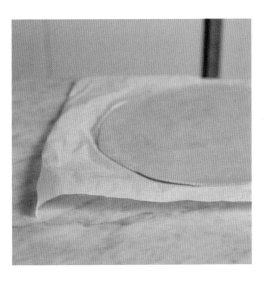

1st rest

After the dough has been mixed, we have our first rest. In the shop, where we work with large batches of dough, the pastry pucks are stored in containers overnight, which is a sufficient length of time for all of the reactions mentioned previously to occur. This timing is going to differ when you execute the recipe at home as the mixing sees less aggravation due to the size of the batch. Less tension has been established so less time is required for it to rest. For your single batch recipe, we are just looking at getting the fats in the dough (butter) set enough to be able to handle.

2nd rest

The second resting stage happens once the dough has been sheeted (or rolled). This is the most crucial rest of the two, particularly if you've foregone a longer rest immediately after mixing. If you have the time and space, we recommend keeping your dough covered on a tray and refrigerated for at least an hour. However, if you feel that the consistency of the pastry is at a point where it can be shaped into the tin, carrying out the second rest of the dough inside the shell (in either the fridge or even freezer) will suffice. Just be sure to let the pastry come back to room temperature before baking.

The advantage of resting flat on paper is that if there is any kind of retraction that may take place after the rather strenuous process of rolling out the pastry, its best to have this happen before it's formed into the final desired shape.

The pastry has now undergone all of the tension-inducing steps of the recipe, and will only need to be pressed into the shell and baked. This last rest gives the established gluten network time to reset and eliminates any potential shrinking in the oven.

Rolling

First, forget everything you know about rolling

The way we roll our dough is the process that has changed the most since the early days of Tarts Anon. From making ten tarts a week in our lowly apartment kitchen in Richmond, up until moving into a shared kitchen in Collingwood, we were rolling every batch out by hand. We continued this up until around the forty tart a week mark, at which point a mate who had a small dough sheeter in his kitchen in Abbotsford helped us out of this tight corner. Working with larger batches of dough means we've adjusted our method for scale, but removing the dough sheeter from the equation to rewrite the recipe for home use made us stop and appreciate how far the dough itself had evolved – and how we could guide you at home.

The key challenge (and the key to shop-grade pastry) is to mimic the actions of a dough sheeter using a rolling pin (ironic, we know) to ensure that the dough is being 'moved' and not stretched.

Rolling out the dough, essentially transforming it from a small thick disc into a large flat disc, seems simple enough, but the way you get there has ramifications. If the dough is taken from its original shape and then stretched into a longer oval,

and then stretched in the other direction to create a circle, you essentially take the original structure of the dough and elongate the gluten network, putting those strands under strain. It will eventually suffer from 'springback', or retraction, which will cause shrinkage when baked.

By starting off in the middle of your dough and rolling outwards, moving toward the edges, you'll maintain relaxed connections within the gluten network, allowing your pastry to keep its intended shape and minimising shrinkage.

Four essential tips for rolling out pastry at home

1 Baking paper
To roll out pastry at home, we recommend sandwiching the pastry between two pieces of baking paper and then using a rolling pin. This will negate the need for adding excess flour, which will in turn dry out the dough and change the composition of the pastry.

2 Release and reattach
You want to ensure that you are moving the pastry, not stretching it. Lifting the baking paper away from either side of the pastry as you roll it is the difference between 'stretching' (continuously rolling out on a surface that is gripping to the underside of your pastry), and 'moving' the pastry (as you gently yet assertively distribute the dough across the surface). Releasing and reattaching the baking paper several times throughout the rolling process will not only make the whole exercise that much easier, it will also give you a much better end result.

Lining

From here, we will be laying the pastry inside the tin as gently as possible, to avoid overstretching the dough. Every movement you make will be directed back towards the centre of the circle of pastry and you should be endeavouring to fit as much of the batch into the tin as humanly possible. By folding the pastry into the corners instead of pushing, we won't stretch it and the established gluten network won't retract away from the centre.

Some tips for lining your tart tin

1   Using the flats of your fingers, pinch the edges of the pastry and push downwards at an angle, pressing all of the dough into the scalloped edge (what we call the 'knuckles') of the tin and reinforcing the edges.

2   Ideally, you'll be left with a very small amount of pastry overhanging the edge of the tart. For what is still overhanging, remove as little as possible with a sharp knife, so as to maximise the height of your shell.

3   Use a slicing motion to cut through the excess pastry instead of cutting, as even the slightest pressure in the wrong direction can add onto any existing tension in the pastry.

3 Move slowly, but assertively
The rolling out of the dough should be a gradual process, which is one of the main reasons why using an automated dough sheeter is so effective. Allowing the dough to be slowly flattened by using assertive movements, and making sure that the dough is maintaining its original composition as much as humanly possible, will keep the dough from wanting to move back towards its starting point when it's in the oven.

4 Roll to size
Roll out your pastry in a circular shape. Constantly rotating the dough circle as you roll will ensure that the shape will remain consistent. When you place the tin on top of your rolled-out pastry, you should have a minimum of 3.5 cm (1½ in) of excess pastry on either side of the base of the tin.

Baking

Everyone has opinions on blind baking methods. Whichever one you choose, it's just as important to have something that won't get damaged through baking (both the lining material and weights) as it is to have something that will conduct the heat and be weighty enough to minimise any potential movement (puffing, slipping etc.).

In Tarts Anon's case, we stumbled across what we believe to be the ultimate blind baking method. In the shop we use metal tart tin inserts (a slightly smaller tart tin, wrapped in foil), which conduct heat into the pastry and that, when packed with rice, are weighty enough that they can keep the crust in its place as it bakes. The invention came about by accident back in the days when we were operating at home. We'd amassed a collection of tart tins by different brands that curiously varied in size despite what they said on the tin – and discovered that one make was the perfect insert for our preferred tin.

Having an insert that can be preheated means the pastry begins to cook immediately and the small pockets of butter we worked to maintain don't melt before the pastry has a chance to cook. This allowed us to both speed up our baking process and ensure consistency.

While we have found this to be the perfect blind-baking method for the shop considering the number of tart shells we bake daily and the consistency we require, a more conventional method of blind-baking will be perfectly adequate for a single tart. Place a sheet of aluminium foil over the pastry, pour rice inside, and press into the scalloped edges and around the edge of the pastry tin to ensure the shape won't change during baking.

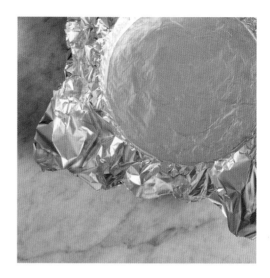

People tend to have varying opinions on what is the best combination of sheet and weight for blind baking, so here's our consideration of this.

Our unsolicited guide to the best blind-baking materials

Sheets
Baking paper is popular, but its tendency to wrinkle and crease is a deterrent, not to mention the difficulty in getting it to fit neatly inside the pastry.

Aluminium foil has similar problems, but has less of a mind of its own than paper – making it a little more on the compliant side. It does have a tendency to stick, however, but this is usually negated by a spritz of oil spray.

Multiple layers of commercial grade cling film certainly won't stick, but it lets itself down in every other department with its tendency to shrink, not to mention the fact that it will release thousands of toxins into the pastry and the oven when you bake it.

Baking weights

When it comes to weights however, there are far too many to mention. Rice, coins, ceramic weights, any kind of dried pulse or bean. We have always been inclined to use rice, but that may have more to do with the fact that it is far and away the most common.

Rice is the smallest of the weights, and will fill gaps better than the larger options – leaving fewer inconsistencies in the pastry.

Dried pulses work well and are almost as cost efficient, but don't fill gaps as well.

Ceramic beads are usually heavier than dried lentils, chickpeas etc., conduct heat well, and are a bit more 'pro'.

Coins, in our experience, only really work for the base. Yes, metal is a brilliant conductor of temperature and will transfer heat to the base of the tin better than any of its competitors. But too many coins are needed to support the edges, and you will only need so many coins before the tin itself weighs a metric tonne. This weight will crush the pastry, making cracks and weak spots in the bottom.

The finished crust

The last hurdle we face lies purely in aesthetics. If there are any blemishes or unsightly edges on the pastry, we remove them using a very sharp microplane after the shell has had time to cool. To do this, once you are able to remove the base from the sides of the tin, take the whole shell out of the tin. Secure the base of your shell with your hand, then use the microplane to file off any rough parts on the edge.

This step, of course, is completely superficial and bordering on unnecessary if you're not too fussed with the visual appeal of your tarts. But if you've completely nailed absolutely every step of this recipe to a point where filing off parts of your pastry is unnecessary, please email us for any openings in the kitchen team.

Glaze and Praise

Glazes have become a staple technique in our kitchen and there are so many reasons why we love them. Firstly, setting agents (such as pectin NH and X58) allow the mixtures to set without relying on ingredients with fat or sugar, which can change the flavour profile. Glazes are also stable unrefrigerated, allowing the finished tart to be served at optimum temperature (room temperature). Also, their use has (almost completely) removed the need for us to use gelatine in our kitchen. Finally, they look great.

Some of the glaze recipes in this book will yield slightly more glaze than you need to cover your tart. We don't love creating excess wastage but the glazes can become very difficult to manage when working with smaller volumes. This is why we will direct you to weigh the correct amount of glaze for each recipe in the method when assembling your tarts. Leftover glaze can be stored in the fridge for around six days.

The process for glazing is different for cake-based and custard-based tarts, so we have outlined both in this section.

Cake Tarts

1 Start with a slightly warm tart so that the glaze can spread across the top of the cake layer.

2 Weigh out the first amount of glaze to melt (as specified in the recipe) and gently warm it in a saucepan, ensuring you stir it frequently to prevent the mix from catching and burning.

3 Place the remaining mixture in a tall measuring jug, which will ensure you can blend the glaze efficiently without incorporating air.

4 Once the first part of the mix is fully melted, pour it into the measuring jug and blend until there are no lumps and the glaze seems glossy and smooth.

5 Quickly and carefully pour the glaze from a little bit of a height into the centre of the cake.

6 Next, pick the tart up and swirl it in a circular motion to encourage the glaze to reach the edges while keeping the layer of glaze as even as possible.

7 Then, tap the tart tin gently but assertively on the bench so that the glaze falls into the cervices between the cake and the shell and keeps a nice dome shape that mirrors the top of the cake.

8 If there are any air bubbles that have formed on top, use a blowtorch or the tip of a knife to pop them.

9 Allow the glaze to set for a few minutes in the fridge so that you can cut clean, crisp slices.

Custard Tarts

1 Start with a slightly cool tart – just under room temperature, but not chilled. The pectin in these glazes can set at room temperature, so they have a tendency to start gelling while they are still quite warm.

2 Bring your glaze to a simmer over low heat. It's a good idea to melt it a little more than the recipe states as some glaze will stick to the inside of the jug while it cools down.

3 Once the glaze has fully melted, pour it into a tall, narrow measuring jug.

4 When you have the glaze in the jug, swirl it around to prevent a skin forming on top just before you pour. The friction inside the jug at this point can be enough to dissolve any rogue pieces of jelly without it thickening too much.

5 Pour in a circular motion starting from the inside and working your way outwards. Pour quickly, but be sure that you save enough to reach the edges.

6 Quickly swirl the tart gently back and forth. This should even out the amount of glaze across the top and cover any unglazed areas.

7 Let this set either at room temperature, or sit it on a nice even shelf in your fridge. It won't take long to set, especially if your custard is cool to begin with. It's best to portion at this point (see page 39).

8 We recommend letting these glazes come to room temperature for serving, as they have a superior mouthfeel to gelatine (in our opinion) – not brittle or gelatinous, but almost jammy – so they are really nice when served a little on the warmer side.

Extra Notes on Glazing

1 If the tart is too warm, the glaze will melt when it lands on the tart, which can cause an uneven set. This may cause the runnier part of the mixture to become a little too firm and jelly like.

2 Different recipes in this book call for different weights of glaze depending on the ingredients, as some may have more fat and require different temperatures to ensure that the mix emulsifies properly.

3 Be sure to keep stirring the glaze as you melt it. As the mixture needs to set into a gel, too high a heat can fry the mix before it has a chance to melt.

4 The taller and narrower the measuring jug, the nicer a vortex you can achieve when blending. This keeps the bubbles out and creates a far smoother and better emulsified glaze.

5 Moving quickly at the blending stage of the process is key to keeping the temperature consistent and preventing the mixture from getting too thick. A thick mixture is easily fixed by gently warming it – whether back in the pot or for short bursts in the microwave.

6 A runny mixture will set flatter – and although this may be ideal for some recipes, you run the risk of exposing parts of the cake layer underneath. Make sure that you don't boil the glaze, as this can throw out the consistency. You can also chill the glaze and start again if you feel as though its too thin to get the finish you want.

7 Pouring the mixture from a height means that the 'puddle' of glaze on top of the tart has a circular shape to begin with. As you tilt and swirl, this means that the amount remains consistent across the top and allows you to get to the scalloped edges of the tart tin quicker.

8 Gently tapping the tart on the top of your counter will help the glaze fall into the gap created by the natural dome of the cake. If your glaze is starting to set and doesn't want to move as fluidly, then it can sometimes be helpful to stop and start again to get that clean flawless look.

9 Before you pour your glaze, check that the top of the custard is clear of any kind of foam. This is best removed before you pour the mix into the shell, but sometimes it can resurface during baking. If your custard is cool and firm enough, you can place a piece of paper towel on top, gently press it onto the surface and peel it off very carefully so that any impurities don't float into your glaze.

10 The best thing about pectin X58 is that it has a great mouthfeel that isn't too gelatinous if used properly. It also sets well at room temperature, so try not to leave it in the fridge for too long.

11 Pectin NH gels can handle acid, so we use them for all glazes containing fruit. Whether its brushed on our poured on, they do set quickly as they will activate in the right conditions at 80–85°C (175–185°F). This applies to pectin X58 gels too.

Sliced to Perfection

'Do you use laser beams to cut your tarts?' is a question we've been asked before. Not quite.

If you've gone through the process of making a tart while following all the techniques and tips in this book, then you're going to want to make sure you don't completely ruin the aesthetics by hacking at it with no plan in mind.

Depending on the filling and composition, we sometimes use up to three different knives to cut a single tart. Even the simplest of tarts are made up of at least two layers, meaning that they have different movements and different textures. Therefore, different levels of force are required to portion the different cross-sections of the tart to produce a clean cut. As indulgent as this may seem, we've come to accept that there is no such thing as a knife that can do it all. Right tool for the right job – etcetera – sorry. Now, obviously this process is not essential to divide the tart into separate pieces, but it will definitely give you nice clean and consistent cuts.

To evenly portion your tart, use the scalloped edge of the tart tin as a guide. This technique has become an integral step in how tarts are portioned at Tarts Anon. We call each scallop a 'knuckle'. The tart tins we use in the shop have sixty-four knuckles, and therefore each slice equates to approximately six-and-a-bit knuckles (we've since custom made a cake divider which marks where the slices should go to speed up the process). It is worth counting the number of knuckles on your tart shell to give you an idea of where you'll need to portion your tarts to get even slices. You might think this isn't exact mathematics (64 knuckles/10 = 6.4 knuckles) and therefore not quite as precise as we profess, but remember that the knife itself has a width (usually around 1 mm), and that knife will not just part the sea, but will take some hostages with it in the form of crumbs.

To make your tarts look the best every time, make sure you take your time with this part of the process. It helps to ensure the tart is at room temperature before you begin to portion it.

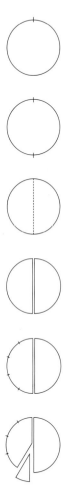

For custard tarts

1 Start by removing the outside of the tart tin, but leave the tart on its base.

2 Take a thin paring knife and, with the forefinger of your non-cutting hand supporting the pastry shell, cut through the crust all the way to the base.

3 Rotate the tart 180° and repeat.

4 Place your kitchen knife in hot water and wipe most of it away, leaving the blade slightly moist. Use the length and sharpness of the blade to slice through the 'skin' on the top of the custard, then use a rocking action to cut through the base.

5 Next, take your paring knife again and mark the edge of the crust to portion into your desired slices. If you're wanting slices to be exact and the same size, we suggest counting the 'knuckles' on the outside of the crust and dividing that number by the number of portions you want (ours are 6.5 knuckles for a 25 cm/10 in tin, for reference). We also make a small mark in the very centre of the tart so that we can have an indicator of where our cuts are going to be directed.

6 Cut into portions by using your hot knife to cut starting from the centre and out to the edge of the crust, ensuring your movement is swift and assertive (and of course, careful). It is important to keep your knife clean throughout this process, as any build-up of custard on the edges of the knife can cause the blade to stick to the skin and tear the surface. Once finished, push the slices back together before serving.

For glazed cake tarts

When portioning cake tarts with a glaze, we follow the same process to that of a custard tart. The glazes are very similar to the custards in that they have a thin 'skin' on the surface, which will need to be sliced through with a hot, sharp and slightly moistened blade. Glazed cake tarts have a soft interior that a sharp knife will cut through easily with a rocking motion.

For cake tarts that are unglazed

For unglazed cake tarts, we use a slightly more complex, but usually more forgiving technique. Once we have made our cuts through the crust with a paring knife, we use a serrated knife to mark the tart in half and to make the initial incisions through the slightly crustier tops of the cake. Then, switch to a chef's knife, which will move more cleanly through the denser, softer part of the cake and through the base.

For tarts that require dusting

For any tarts that are dusted (e.g. with cocoa powder) as a final step, we recommend doing so after the tart has been portioned and the slices are pushed back together. This protects the cut surfaces of the tarts and will give a nice and clean appearance.

The Tarts

Classic
Tarts

Tarts themselves are a classic dessert, steeped in history and nostalgia.

The advent of the modern tart can be traced back to the recipes published in the fourteenth-century English cookbook *The Forme of Cury*. At the time, tarts were a way to show off the colourful fruits and custards that pastry chefs were so fond of – all within a single entity. And life got more exciting than ever in the fifteenth and sixteenth centuries, when the first written recipes for puff and shortcrust pastry began to emerge.

One of the greatest things about reinventing a classic dish is working out what made it classic in the first place and applying new techniques to (hopefully) make it the best version of itself. Some of the tarts in this chapter are our spin on classic flavours that you'll be more than familiar with (vanilla custard, plain old lemon, etc.). Some are simply 'classics' from the Tarts Anon menu. What makes a Tarts Anon classic? It's a tart that comes back on the menu over and over again, usually due to popularity.

The majority of the tarts on our menu are based on familiar flavour combinations, enhanced by considered pastry and baking techniques. We've combined traditional recipes and flavours with a modern and (you'll come to know) a rather meticulous methodology. No part of the recipe is superfluous or done 'just because that's the way it's done'. The recipes in this section are also the building blocks for the tarts in later chapters where we've explored a number of bolder flavour combinations and used some more sophisticated techniques.

Basically, these tarts are people pleasers. Classics that have stood the test of time and also classics that are repeatedly requested each month when we release a new menu in the shop.

If you're not sure where to start with your tart making, then we suggest starting here.

Vanilla Custard Tart

This has to be the most classic of the classics. There's something so satisfying about a vanilla custard that cannot be surpassed. The two things you need to nail for the perfect vanilla custard tart are the texture of the custard and showcasing the taste of the vanilla. Gareth is heavily influenced by Heston Blumenthal's approach to cookery, particularly his scientific approach to combining flavours to enhance one another. One of Heston's hacks is combining vanilla with a small amount of coffee to add a certain 'robustness' to the vanilla flavour. We've also used soft brown sugar in this recipe to really lean into the warming, rich, dried fruit notes of Madagascan vanilla.

475 g (1 lb 1 oz) pouring (whipping) cream
55 g (2 oz) double (heavy) cream
40 g (1½ oz) cream cheese
6 g (¼ oz) vanilla paste or 1 vanilla bean
1 g coffee beans

140 g (5 oz) soft brown sugar
195 g (7 oz) egg yolk
1 × baked Shortcrust Pastry shell (page 23)
nutmeg, for grating

Preheat the oven to 125°C (255°F).

Add the creams, cream cheese, vanilla, coffee beans and brown sugar to a saucepan over medium heat. Bring to a simmer, then remove from heat immediately.

To temper the egg yolks, add them to a mixing bowl and whisk in a small amount of the hot cream mixture until well incorporated. Then add the remaining cream mixture and whisk again until combined. Using a hand-held blender, blend until the mixture is shiny and smooth, keeping the head of the blender submerged so that no air gets into the mix. Strain the mixture through a sieve into a jug to use straight away – you want to keep it as warm as possible to ensure that the mixture cooks evenly in the oven.

Place the prepared shell in the oven. Pour the custard into the shell until it is full to the brim. Bake for 30 minutes, or until the custard is slightly wobbly in the centre, then remove from the oven and allow to cool in the shell.

Once the custard has completely cooled, remove the tart from the tin and portion into slices with a hot, sharp knife (see page 39). Finish by grating a fine layer of nutmeg on top before serving.

Plain Old Lemon Tart

One of the first tarts we had on the Tarts Anon menu was the Lemon and Rhubarb Tart (see the variation below). It was insanely popular, but people still asked for a plain lemon tart. 'No way' we always said, because we genuinely believed the Lemon and Rhubarb was superior. One day we relented and decided to have a go at what Cat called the 'Plain Old Lemon Tart', named as a bit of a jab. Lo and behold, the result reminded us how great a simple but well-executed lemon tart truly is, so we admitted defeat and now it's one of the staples on the menu. Be warned, though, while the method and ingredient lists are short, this is the tart that causes the most stress amongst our kitchen staff, Gareth included. It's temperamental, fragile, and a little difficult to work with. But it's also fragrant, zingy and the perfect balance of creamy sweetness and sour refreshment.

185 g (6½ oz) lemon juice
10 g (¼ oz) lemon zest
130 g (4½ oz) pouring (whipping) cream
150 g (5½ oz) double (heavy) cream
250 g (9 oz) caster (superfine) sugar

95 g (3¼ oz) egg
220 g (8 oz) egg yolk
70 g (2½ oz) Dulce de Leche (page 139)
1 × baked Shortcrust Pastry shell (page 23)

Preheat the oven to 125°C (255°F).

Add the lemon juice and zest, creams and sugar to a saucepan over medium heat. Bring to a simmer then immediately remove from heat. To temper the whole eggs and egg yolks, add them to a mixing bowl and whisk in a small amount of the hot cream mixture until well incorporated. Then add the remaining cream mixture and whisk again until combined. Using a hand-held blender, blend until the mixture is shiny and smooth, keeping the head of the blender submerged so that no air gets into the mix. Strain the custard into a jug and let sit for 10 minutes for any impurities to rise to the top, then skim them off with a ladle.

In the meantime, spread the dulce de leche over the base of the baked pastry shell. This will provide a protective layer between the custard mix and the shell, ensuring it stays crisp. Once the surface is clear of bubbles, place the prepared shell in the oven. Pour the warm custard into the tart shell straight away to ensure that the mixture cooks evenly in the oven.

Bake for 30 minutes, or until the custard is slightly wobbly in the centre, then remove from the oven and allow to cool.

Once the custard has completely cooled, remove the tart from the tin and portion into slices with a hot, sharp knife (see page 39).

Lemon and Rhubarb Tart Variation
Spread a layer of Rhubarb compote (see page 133) over the base of the pastry shell before pouring the custard on top.

Fig and Honey Tart

Although figs and honey are such a solid flavour combination, it was quite by coincidence that these ingredients worked their way into one of our tarts. Our front of house team put in an order for honey because people were asking for some in their coffee (I know, right?) but the supplier accidentally sent over a beautiful leatherwood honey. It was way too good to waste in lattes and flat whites, so we decided to use it in a tart. It was the middle of fig season, and we were lucky to get our hands on plump figs in a box lined with their own leaves. This tart is nothing too fancy: we're simply replacing some of the sugar in the frangipane with honey and highlighting the beauty of the fig. Use up any 'less than perfect' figs in the fig jam underneath. If you can get your hands on fig leaves, follow the recipe to create the fig leaf powder for finishing. It's a very nice (but very optional) way to elevate the tart due to the lovely coconutty flavour of fig leaves.

1 × baked Shortcrust Pastry shell (page 23)
3 large figs, cut into quarters

Fig leaf powder (optional)
100 g (3½ oz) fig leaves
icing (confectioners') sugar
2 g citric acid

Fig jam
1 kg (2 lb 3 oz) figs
400 g (14 oz) caster (superfine) sugar,
    plus 160 g (5½ oz)
20 g (¾ oz) pectin jaune

15 g (½ oz) citric acid
40 g (1½ oz) water

Honey cake batter
140 g (5 oz) natural almond meal
75 g (2¾ oz) plain (all-purpose) flour
3 g (0.1 oz) baking powder
2 g salt
160 g (5½ oz) egg
130 g (4½ oz) leatherwood honey
80 g (2¾ oz) caster (superfine) sugar
160 g (5½ oz) Brown butter (page 111)

Preheat the oven to 65°C (150°F).

Fig leaf powder
Arrange the fig leaves on a tray lined with baking paper, then leave to dry in the preheated oven overnight. In the morning, or when the leaves have fully dried, remove from the oven and allow to cool. Place the leaves in a blender together with the sugar and the citric acid and blitz until it forms a fine and slightly green-tinged powder. Reserve the powder in a tightly sealed container to prevent it from going sticky and lumpy.

Fig jam
Place the figs in a blender and blitz into a smooth puree. This can also be made with larger pieces of fig that are cooked until they collapse, however for the ease of spreading, we go for blended.

A shop-bought fig puree can also work quite well, but usually doesn't give the same colour as one that has been made fresh.

Put the fig puree, or the collapsed figs, in a saucepan and mix with 400 g (14 oz) of the sugar. Allow the mixture to come to the boil over medium–high heat while whisking continuously, as it will tend to stick to the bottom of the pan. Take the remaining sugar and mix with the pectin. Rain this into the boiling fig mixture and continue to cook until it reaches 106°C (225°F), or until the bubbles grow larger and the mixture has thickened. Once the jam has reached this point, mix the citric acid with the water in a separate bowl until the granules have fully dissolved. Add this to the jam and return to the boil. Pour this mix into a container and allow to set. →

Honey cake batter

Weigh the dry ingredients, except the sugar, in a bowl and stir together. Add the eggs, honey and sugar to a separate mixing bowl. Either with a whisk or a stand mixer fitted with a whisk attachment, slowly combine until the sugar and honey have dissolved. You do not want to incorporate any air at this stage, as the batter tends to separate when the butter is added and forms a foamy crust, so keep the speed low.

Melt the brown butter in a saucepan. You want this to be warm enough so that the liquid doesn't cool down too quickly, but cool enough so that it doesn't develop any burnt characteristics. If the butter is too hot, it can also fry the egg mixture as you add it, so a thermometer is useful (we aim for roughly 100°C/210°F).

Once the butter comes up to temperature, slowly pour it into the egg and sugar mixture (or add little by little, if whisking by hand). Ensure that the mixture is well emulsified, as this will prevent the butter from bleeding out later, giving the cake a greasy texture. Finally, mix in the dry ingredients, making sure that there are no lumps suspended throughout the batter.

To assemble and bake

To assemble the tart, spread 150 g (5½ oz) of fig jam in an even layer over the base of the pastry shell. Then pour 650 g (1 lb 7 oz) of the honey batter on top and allow to cool slightly. Once the batter has firmed up a touch, slice the figs into quarters and arrange evenly around the top of the cake. We try to have ten evenly placed pieces for the tarts sold in store to ensure that every slice has a piece of fig in the centre. Bake the tart in the oven for approximately 30 minutes, or until the crust is an even golden brown and the centre of the tart is firm. Remove from the oven and allow to cool inside the tin.

Once the tart has completely cooled, remove it from the tin. Portion the tart into slices (see page 39) and dust with a light coating of fig leaf sugar, if using.

Chocolate and Hazelnut Tart

Chocolate and hazelnut is a very familiar flavour profile to most, but its potential goes far beyond Ferrero Rocher, Kinder Buenos and Nutella. We initially started working on this tart for a Valentine's Day collaboration with our friend and baker, Miss Trixie Drinks Tea, but soon realised it was too delicious (and popular) to keep it out of the regular rotation of tarts in the shop. Using quality ingredients is key here as there are not many variables at work: a nice praline, chocolate, salt, sugar, cream and eggs.

1 × baked Shortcrust Pastry shell (page 23)
100 g (3½ oz) Dulce de Leche (page 139)

Hazelnut praline paste
80 g (2¾ oz) hazelnuts
80 g (2¾ oz) caster (superfine) sugar

Chocolate hazelnut custard
560 g (1 lb 4 oz) pouring (whipping) cream
3 g (0.1 oz) salt
65 g (2¼ oz) caster (superfine) sugar
240 g (8½ oz) egg yolk
145 g (5 oz) dark chocolate (70% cocoa solids), callets or buttons

Preheat the oven to 165°C (330°F).

Spread the dulce de leche on the bottom of the pastry shell in a smooth even layer.

Hazelnut praline paste
Roast the hazelnuts on a baking tray (sheet) for approximately 15 minutes. Once they are a medium golden brown, remove them from the oven and set aside. If your hazelnuts still have skin on them, pour them onto a tea towel (dish towel) while still hot, gather the corners together, and roll them around inside the towel to loosen the skins. Shake the hazelnuts out of the towel to separate them from the skin. Put a pot on the stove and gently melt the sugar over a low heat. Continue to cook until the caramel becomes deep brown, then add the warm hazelnuts. Stir to coat the nuts in the caramel, then tip onto a tray to cool slightly, just until they are warm.

Place the warm hazelnuts into a food processor and blend until the oil starts to come out of the nuts and the mixture becomes a smooth paste, then decant into a container.

Chocolate hazelnut custard
Add the cream, salt, sugar and the hazelnut praline paste to a saucepan over medium heat. Bring to a simmer, while whisking, then remove from the heat immediately. To temper the egg yolks, add them to a mixing bowl and whisk in a small amount of the hot cream mixture until well incorporated. Add the chocolate to a large bowl, then add a small amount of the hot cream-praline mixture and whisk to combine. Add the remaining mixture and use a hand-held blender to blend until the mixture is shiny and smooth – to prevent any air from being incorporated into the mix, keep the head of the blender underneath the surface. Decant into a jug to use straight away – you want to keep it as warm as possible to ensure the mixture cooks evenly in the oven.

To bake
Place the prepared tart shell into the oven, then pour the custard over the dulce de leche layer. Bake for 30 minutes, or until the custard is slightly wobbly in the centre, then remove from the oven and allow to cool.

Once the custard has completely cooled, remove the tart from the tin and portion into slices using a hot, sharp knife (see page 39).

Chocolate and Caramel Tart

Back in 2015, a good friend and role model asked Gareth to develop a recipe for a gastro pub menu. The brief? 'A brilliant chocolate tart.' This is what came out. It was the first item we put on the Tarts Anon menu (along with our Cherry and Almond Tart, page 59) and it gained instant popularity. We see can why – it's a superbly well-balanced tart that is decadent without being overwhelming. It gained a cult following during Melbourne's lockdown of 2020 and on the weeks we didn't have it as part of our rotating menu, our customers were vocal in their disappointment. The escalation was such that Catherine started trying to tell people the tart 'wasn't even that good' to encourage them to order something else. But we have to admit this tart is a true classic and probably *is* that good.

1 × baked Shortcrust Pastry shell (page 23)
cocoa powder, for dusting

Salted caramel
270 g (9½ oz) Dulce de Leche (page 139)
2 g salt

Chocolate custard
560 g (1 lb 4 oz) pouring (whipping) cream
3 g (0.1 oz) salt
65 g (2¼ oz) caster (superfine) sugar
240 g (8½ oz) egg yolk
145 g dark chocolate (70% cocoa solids),
    callets or buttons

Preheat the oven to 125°C (255°F).

Salted caramel
Using a metal spoon, remove the dulce de leche from the tin (this is how we do it in the shop as it saves you buying a new rubber spatula every week – the metal spoon gives you the rigidity to be able to scoop the caramel, but also won't be damaged by the sharp metal edges on the top of the can). Now, using a spatula, wooden spoon or kitchen stand mixer, work in the salt until smooth – ensuring not to over work the mixture. The more you mix, the more you will break down the protein structure developed through the cooking of the condensed milk. Then, use a palette knife to spread an even layer of caramel onto the base of your cooled pastry shell.

Chocolate custard
Place the cream, salt and sugar in a saucepan over medium heat. Bring to a simmer, then remove from heat immediately. To temper the egg yolks, add them to a mixing bowl and whisk in a small amount of the hot cream mixture until well incorporated. Add the remaining cream mixture and whisk again until combined.

Add the chocolate to a large bowl, then add a small amount of the hot cream mixture and whisk to combine. Add the remaining mixture, and then use a hand-held blender to blend until shiny and smooth – to prevent any air from being incorporated into the mix, keep the head of the blender underneath the surface. Decant into a jug to use straight away – you want to keep it as warm as possible to ensure the mixture cooks evenly in the oven.

To bake
Place the prepared tart into the oven, then pour the custard on top of the caramel layer. Bake for 30 minutes, or until the custard is slightly wobbly in the centre, then remove from the oven and allow to cool.

Once the custard has completely cooled, remove from the tin and portion into slices with a hot, sharp knife (see page 39). Dust each slice with a light coating of cocoa powder to finish.

Cherry and Almond Tart

This tart is based on a cherry and hazelnut financier recipe that Gareth used to make some seventeen years ago as an apprentice chef at Sydney's acclaimed (though now-closed) Pier restaurant. It inspired one of the first tarts we made for Tarts Anon at home and will always be on our rotating menu. It's forever Gareth's favourite: he loves how the savoury, buttery notes in the frangipane and the pastry are offset by the sweet and sour bursts of cherry throughout. It's super simple and when made well it's just the perfect pastry to have with a coffee or as a standalone dessert.

1 × baked Shortcrust Pastry shell (page 23)
icing (confectioners') sugar, for dusting

Sour cherries
1 × 680 g (1½ lb) jar of sour cherries
(to yield 200 g/7 oz drained sour cherries, plus reserved liquid)
caster (superfine) sugar, see method
citric acid, see method

Almond cake batter
140 g (5 oz) natural almond meal
75 g (2¾ oz) plain (all-purpose) flour
3 g (0.1 oz) baking powder
2 g salt
160 g (5½ oz) egg
185 g (6½ oz) caster (superfine) sugar
160 g (5½ oz) Brown butter (page 111)

Preheat the oven to 165°C (330°F).

Sour cherries
Strain the sour cherries from the jar, reserving the liquid. For every 100 g (3½ oz) of the cherry liquid, measure out 60 g (2 oz) of sugar and 2 g of citric acid. Add the sugar and citric acid to a saucepan with the cherry liquid, bring to a simmer over medium heat, then stir together to ensure the sugar has dissolved. Remove from the heat and set aside to cool. (This can also be done with the same amount of fresh pitted cherries by replacing the cherry liquid with water and poaching the de-seeded cherries in the syrup until they are soft.) Pour this liquid over the jarred cherries and let sit in the syrup for at least 3–4 hours before using.

Almond cake batter
Weigh the dry ingredients, except the sugar, in a bowl and stir together. Add the eggs and sugar to a separate mixing bowl. Either with a whisk or a stand mixer fitted with the whisk attachment, slowly combine until the sugar has dissolved. You do not want to incorporate any air at this stage, as it tends to separate when the butter is added and forms a foamy crust, so keep the speed low.

Gently melt the brown butter in a saucepan. You want it to be warm enough so that the liquid doesn't cool down too quickly, but cool enough so that it doesn't develop any burnt characteristics. If the butter is too hot, it can also fry the egg mixture as you add it, so a thermometer is useful (we aim for roughly 100°C/210°F).

Once the butter comes up to temperature, slowly pour it into the egg and sugar mixture (or add little by little, if whisking by hand). The mixture must be well emulsified, as this will ensure that the butter doesn't bleed out later and give the cake a greasy texture. Finally, mix in the dry ingredients, ensuring that there are no lumps suspended throughout the batter. →

To assemble and bake

Pour a thin layer of almond batter (approximately one-third of the quantity) into a prepared pastry shell to cover the base. (This will keep the cherries in place when adding the remaining batter). Then, strain off 200 g (7 oz) of the marinated sour cherries (see previous page) through a sieve and discard the liquid. Blot the fruit on some paper towels, then arrange them over the batter in four concentric circles, with a gap of roughly 1 cm (½ in) in between each circle and in between each cherry.

Pour the remaining batter over the top of the cherries and push any floating cherries under the surface. Place the tart into the oven to bake for approximately 30 minutes, or until the crust is an even golden brown and the centre of the tart is firm. Remove from the oven and allow to cool inside the tin.

Once the cake layer has completely cooled, remove the tart from the tin. Portion into slices (see page 39) and dust with a light coating of icing sugar.

Festive and spiced plum variations

At Christmas, we like to turn this into a festive Cherry and Gingerbread Tart variation by adding 6 g (0.2 oz) of mixed spice and 3 g (0.1 oz) of ground ginger. You can also make this tart with plums, which is what we originally did before switching to cherry (Gareth claimed making the plum tart for our first Christmas offering was 'the worst day of his life' – he spent hours slicing kilos and kilos of plums from our local grocer, half of which were spoiled – making it literally the pits). If you're only making one though, you (probably) won't end up scarred and, unlike Gareth, will find it quite easy. Just substitute cherries for 250 g (9 oz) plums, pitted and cut into approx. 1.5 cm (½ in) slices.

Carrot Cake Tart

This tart-ified version of a carrot cake might not be an obvious classic, but it belongs in this chapter as a great foundational recipe for the tarts in our 'Not Your Average Tarts' chapter. The cream cheese glaze is what makes this one special – it's designed to taste the same as a typical cream cheese frosting and to sit perfectly flat across the top of the tart (and it's texturally superior as well, if we say so ourselves). You can, of course, with some practice, use a palette knife to get frosting perfectly flat, but at the scale we make tarts, we needed to find a way to make this as consistent as possible. The cake itself is, we believe, the perfect carrot cake: spicy, nutty and, of course, carrot-y.

1 × baked Shortcrust Pastry shell (page 23)

Cream cheese glaze
60 g (2 oz) caster (superfine) sugar
1 g salt
3 g (0.1 oz) pectin X58
130 g (4½ oz) cream cheese
1 g orange zest
100 g (3½ oz) milk

Carrot cake batter
130 g (4½ oz) grated carrot
    (from approx. 2 carrots)
20 g (¾ oz) natural almond meal
95 g (3¼ oz) walnut meal
70 g (2½ oz) plain (all-purpose) flour
4 g (0.14 oz) baking powder
5 g (0.2 oz) salt
220 g (8 oz) soft brown sugar
100 g (3½ oz) egg
100 g Brown butter (page 111)

Preheat the oven to 165°C (210°F).

Cream cheese glaze
First mix the sugar, salt and pectin in a small bowl and set aside. Put the cream cheese into a plastic measuring jug and soften briefly in the microwave. Add the orange zest and milk to a saucepan and bring to a simmer over medium heat. Add the sugar and pectin mix to the simmering milk and whisk to combine, then remove from heat. Strain the milk mixture through a fine sieve into the jug with the cream cheese, then blend until smooth with a hand-held blender. Pour into a container, cover with a piece of plastic wrap placed directly onto the surface of the frosting and leave to cool in the fridge.

Carrot cake batter
Mix the grated carrot with all the dry ingredients, except the sugar, in a bowl and set aside. Add the eggs and sugar to a separate mixing bowl. Either with a whisk or a stand mixer fitted with a whisk attachment, slowly combine until the

sugar has dissolved. You do not want to incorporate any air at this stage, as it tends to separate when the butter is added and forms a foamy crust, so keep the speed low. Melt the brown butter in a saucepan. You want this to be warm enough so that the liquid doesn't cool down too quickly, but cool enough so that it doesn't develop any burnt characteristics. If the butter is too hot, it can also fry the egg mixture as you add it, so a thermometer is useful (we aim for roughly 100°C/210°F).

Once the butter comes up to temperature, slowly pour it into the egg and sugar mixture (or add little by little, if whisking by hand). Ensure that the mixture is well emulsified, as this will prevent the butter from bleeding out later, giving the cake a greasy texture. Then mix in the dry ingredients, making sure that there are no lumps suspended throughout the batter. →

To bake

Pour the batter into your cooled pastry shell and place in the oven to bake for approximately 30 minutes, or until the centre of the tart springs back when pressed. Remove from the oven and allow to cool inside the tin.

To glaze

Once the cake layer has completely cooled it's ready to be glazed (see page 34). Warm two-thirds of the glaze in a small saucepan over low heat until just melted. Pour this onto the remaining third and blend with a hand-held blender until smooth. Pour the glaze onto the centre of the cake and use a swirling motion to move the glaze to the edges of the tart. Then, tap gently on the bench so that the glaze fills the knuckles of the crust.

Once the glaze has filled the gaps, allow to set for 20 minutes before removing the tart from the tin and portioning into slices with a hot, sharp knife (see page 39).

Smoked Pecan and Butterscotch Tart

This is a reformatted version of the pecan pie. We honestly believe – unless you grew up eating them (which not many people in Australia did) – that pecan pies are really not very nice (sorry). This tart, on the other hand, is undeniably very nice. Gareth set it as a pressure test for an elimination challenge on *MasterChef Australia* in 2022 and it's been one of our most popular tarts ever since. Some people criticised it for not being complex enough for a pressure test, but they hadn't baked it or eaten it. The execution required at every step and the final aesthetic are what sets it apart from other tarts, as of course does its taste. To really make this tart great (and it *is* intended to be great), ensure you take every element to its deepest colour without burning.

1 × baked Shortcrust Pastry shell (page 23)
whole pecan nuts, to decorate

Caramel
120 g (4½ oz) pouring (whipping) cream
280 g (10 oz) caster (superfine) sugar
130 g (4½ oz) butter
160 g (5½ oz) milk
16 g (½ oz) salt
125 g (4½ oz) Dulce de Leche (page 139)

Smoked maple glaze
120 g (4½ oz) soft brown sugar
5 g (0.2 oz) pectin NH
2 g smoke powder, or a couple of drops
    of liquid smoke
100 g (3½ oz) water
200 g (7 oz) maple syrup
2 g citric acid

Pecan puree
150 g (5½ oz) pecans

Pecan cake batter
125 g (4½ oz) natural almond meal
45 g (1½ oz) plain (all-purpose) flour
3 g (0.1 oz) baking powder
4 g (0.14 oz) salt
85 g (3 oz) Pecan puree, above
90 g (3 oz) golden caster (superfine) sugar
80 g (2¾ oz) soft brown sugar
145 g (5 oz) egg
80 g (2¾ oz) Brown butter (page 111)

Preheat the oven to 165°C (330°F).

Caramel
Warm the cream slightly in a saucepan over medium–low heat and set aside. Place the sugar, butter, milk and salt and in a pan and bring to a gentle simmer over medium heat. Continue to cook while whisking, to ensure it doesn't burn, and let the liquid reduce until the mixture becomes thick and caramelised (approximately 145°C/295°F). At this point, remove the caramel from the stove and add the warmed cream, then whisk to combine. Give it a quick blitz with a hand-held blender until shiny, then allow

to cool. Then, weigh out 125 g (4½ oz) of the caramel, mix with the dulce de leche and store in a container.

Smoked maple glaze
Weigh the sugar, pectin and smoke powder in a bowl. Then, add the water and maple syrup to a saucepan and bring to a boil over medium–high heat. Once boiling, rain the sugar mixture into the maple syrup while whisking. →

Lastly, add the citric acid and boil again, simmering for a minute or so to properly hydrate the pectin. Blend with a hand-held blender until smooth and glossy then decant into a container to allow to set before using.

Pecan puree
Toast the pecans on a baking tray (sheet) for about 15 minutes, or until deep golden brown. Whilst still warm, blend the nuts in a food processor until smooth and runny. Set this mixture aside.

Pecan cake batter
Weigh the dry ingredients, except the sugars, in a separate bowl and stir them together. Add the eggs and sugar to a separate mixing bowl. Either with a whisk or a stand mixer fitted with a whisk attachment, slowly combine until the sugar has dissolved. You do not want to incorporate any air at this stage, as it tends to separate when the butter is added and forms a foamy crust, so keep the speed low.

Melt the brown butter in a saucepan. You want this to be warm enough so that the liquid doesn't cool down too quickly, but cool enough so that it doesn't develop any burnt characteristics. If the butter is too hot, it can also fry the egg mixture as you add it, so a thermometer is useful (we aim for roughly 100°C/210°F).

Once the butter comes up to temperature, slowly pour it into the egg and sugar mixture (or add little by little, if whisking by hand). Ensure that the mixture is well emulsified, as this will prevent the butter from bleeding out later, giving the cake a greasy texture. Then mix in the dry ingredients, making sure that there are no lumps suspended throughout the batter.

To bake
Spread 250 g (9 oz) of the caramel over the base of the tart shell, then pour 650 g (1 lb 7 oz) of batter on top. Arrange the pecans on top of the tart in three concentric circles (we arrange them into ten groups of a 3–2–1 formation so that every slice gets 6 pecans).

Place the tart into the oven to bake for approximately 30 minutes, or until the crust is an even colour and the centre of the tart is firm. Remove from the oven and allow to cool inside the tin.

To glaze
Once the tart has cooled, it's ready to be glazed (see page 34). Bring the smoked maple glaze to a boil in a small saucepan. Using a large pastry brush, brush a thick layer over the top of the tart and allow to set for a few minutes. Once the glaze is nice and firm, remove the tart from the tin and portion into slices with a hot, sharp knife (see page 39).

Rhubarb Bakewell Tart

A traditional Bakewell is made with shortcrust pastry, a layer of fruit jam and a layer of frangipane that is topped with flaked almonds and icing. This tart-ified version uses rhubarb instead of more traditional strawberry or cherry jam, simply because we had some in the fridge at the time. This recipe calls for you to make your jam more like a thick compote, which is a great way to highlight the fruit, but really the key to making this tart excellent is to nail the cook on the cake. If the cake itself isn't right then you'll end up with something too sloppy or too dry, and we guarantee the compote won't save you. Look for a nice firmness to the cake, but not so much that it springs back. If you want to use a skewer to test the doneness of your cake, keep in mind that you want it to come out with a little residue on it – just not so much that it's sticky. This will ensure your cake still has some moisture to it.

1 × baked Shortcrust Pastry shell (page 23)
120 g (4½ oz) diced almonds

Rhubarb jam
500 g (1 lb 2 oz) rhubarb
200 g (7 oz) caster (superfine) sugar,
    plus 200 g (7 oz)
250 g (9 oz) water, plus 10 g (¼ oz)
7 g (¼ oz) pectin jaune
7 g (¼ oz) citric acid

Almond cake batter
140 g (5 oz) natural almond meal
75 g (2¾ oz) plain (all-purpose) flour
3 g (0.1 oz) baking powder
2 g salt
185 g (6½ oz) caster (superfine) sugar
160 g (5½ oz) egg
160 g (5½ oz) Brown butter (page 111)

Preheat the oven to 165°C (330°F).

Rhubarb jam
Start by cutting the rhubarb into small pieces. Heat 200 g (7 oz) of the sugar and 250 g (9 oz) of the water in a pot on the stove. Bring to a boil, then pour in the rhubarb. Once the syrup comes back to a boil, remove the rhubarb with a slotted spoon, leaving the syrup in the pot. Add the drained rhubarb to a baking tray (sheet) lined with baking paper. Place in the oven to bake for 15 minutes, or until all the liquid has evaporated and the rhubarb looks dry.

Bring the syrup back to the boil once the rhubarb has finished baking then mix the remaining 200 g (7 oz) of sugar with the pectin. Rain this into the boiling syrup and continue to cook until it reaches 107°C (225°F) on the thermometer. Mix the citric acid and the remaining 10 g (¼ oz) of water together, then whisk this along with the

rhubarb into the syrup. Once fully combined, set aside in a container until cool.

Almond cake batter
Weigh the dry ingredients, except the sugar, in a bowl and stir them together. Add the eggs and sugar to a separate mixing bowl. Either with a whisk or a stand mixer fitted with a whisk attachment, slowly combine until the sugar has dissolved. You do not want to incorporate any air at this stage, as it tends to separate when the butter is added and forms a foamy crust, so keep the speed low.

Melt the brown butter in a saucepan. You want this to be warm enough so that the liquid doesn't cool down too quickly, but cool enough so that it doesn't develop any burnt characteristics. If the butter is too hot, it can also fry the egg mixture as you add it, so a thermometer is useful (we aim for roughly 100°C/210°F). →

Once the butter comes up to temperature, slowly pour it into the egg and sugar mixture (or add little by little, if whisking by hand). Ensure that the mixture is well emulsified, as this will prevent the butter from bleeding out later, giving the cake a greasy texture. Then mix in the dry ingredients, making sure that there are no lumps suspended throughout the batter.

To assemble and bake

Spread 150 g (5½ oz) of rhubarb jam over the base of the pastry shell.

Pour the batter over the top of the jam, then sprinkle over the diced almonds to form an even layer. Place the tart into the oven to bake for approximately 30 minutes, or until the crust is an even golden brown and the centre of the tart is firm. Remove from the oven and allow to cool inside the tin.

Once the cake layer has completely cooled, remove from the tin and portion the tart into slices using a hot, sharp knife (see page 39). Finish each slice with a light coating of icing sugar.

Signature Pear Tart

This is the tart that started it all in lockdown, before Tarts Anon even existed. It's the bake that made us think 'Maybe we should sell these?' It's quite a simple tart in its conception: layers of pear and frangipane baked in a shortcrust pastry shell. This tart was inspired by one of the first dishes Gareth ever made as a chef – a frangipane and plum tart, we've simply switched the plums for pears. You can serve this with the bells and whistles if you want (vanilla ice cream or cream), but we genuinely believe this tart is perfect as it is.

1 × baked Shortcrust Pastry shell (page 23)
3 green packham pears
icing (confectioners' sugar), for dusting

Almond cake batter
140 g (5 oz) natural almond meal

75 g (2¾ oz) plain (all-purpose) flour
3 g (0.1 oz) baking powder
2 g salt
185 g (6½ oz) caster (superfine) sugar
160 g (5½ oz) egg
160 g (5½ oz) Brown butter (page 111)

Preheat the oven to 165°C (330°F).

Use an apple corer to remove the core from two of the pears and slice thinly, lengthways, on a sharp mandolin. Cut the third pear into quarters lengthways and use a knife to cut the core out.

Almond cake batter
Weigh the dry ingredients, except the sugar, in a bowl and stir together. Add the eggs and sugar to a separate mixing bowl. Either with a whisk or a stand mixer fitted with a whisk attachment, slowly combine until the sugar has dissolved. You do not want to incorporate any air at this stage, as it tends to separate when the butter is added and forms a foamy crust, so keep the speed low.

Melt the brown butter in a saucepan. You want this to be warm enough so that the liquid doesn't cool down too quickly, but cool enough so that it doesn't develop any burnt characteristics. If the butter is too hot, it can also fry the egg mixture as you add it, so a thermometer is useful (we aim for roughly 100°C/210°F).

Once the butter comes up to temperature, slowly pour it into the egg and sugar mixture (or add little by little, if whisking by hand). Ensure that the mixture is well emulsified, as this will prevent the butter from bleeding out later, giving the cake a greasy texture. Finally, mix in the dry ingredients, making sure that there are no lumps suspended throughout the batter.

To assemble and bake
Pour a thin layer of the almond batter (approx. one-third of the recipe) into the pastry shell. Arrange the slices of pear in an overlapping layer over the batter, then pour another thin layer of almond batter over the top of this. It is important to work quickly at this time as the batter will stiffen as it cools. Add a second layer of pear and then a final layer of batter.

Once the last of the batter is inside the pastry shell, use a mandolin to carefully slice the quartered pear into slightly thicker pieces and arrange 10 pieces on top so they fan out with the pointed ends of the pear facing the centre.

Place the tart into the oven and bake for approximately 30 minutes, or until the crust is an even golden brown and the centre of the tart is firm. Remove from the oven and allow to cool inside the tin.

Once cooled, remove the tart from the tin. Portion the tart into slices with a sharp knife (see page 39) and dust lightly with icing sugar.

Not Your Average Tarts

This collection is dedicated to the most
'Tarts Anon' of tarts – the recipes that gave
us our reputation for out of the box tarts.

Many of these showcase Gareth's background in fine dining, demonstrating techniques and skills that aren't necessarily synonymous with tart baking and might not be known to the home cook. Nonetheless, they should be achievable with the right equipment, time and ingredients if you follow the recipes correctly.

While baking classic tarts never gets old, experimenting with technique and pushing the boundaries of a typical retail pastry shop by using elevated techniques is something that keeps baking interesting and playful. It also keeps people coming back to the shop. While we never claim to be reinventing the wheel, at Tarts Anon we've worked hard to get our processes right through rigorous testing. Setting pectin glazes on top of baked custard tarts may have been done before, but we like to think that this practice – particularly at the scale at which we do it – is unique to us.

But in the same way some more classic recipes require a good understanding of the ingredients, these more technically complex tarts require an understanding of a few different challenges in pastry making. In this chapter we rely on a few lesser-known ingredients: pectin X58 (used to set dairy-based glazes) and pectin NH (to set non-dairy based glazes). These two ingredients make it possible for us to add additional layers to our tarts without it looking or tasting like some aftermarket addition. These pectins set at room temperature, which is perfect for tarts that are baked fresh daily and not refrigerated for any longer than 15 minutes. We also tackle a few different methods that wouldn't necessarily feature in conventional tart making like baking custard on top of a cake layer, how to soak cakes and putting extra layers of biscuits into your pastry and gluing them all together.

These are the tarts that people will remember you for, for better or worse.

Blackberry and Orange Cheesecake Tart

This tart has seen more evolutions than any other tart on the Tarts Anon menu, but the final recipe eventually became the basis for all our other cheesecake-based tarts. Please be warned: this is not a cheesecake. You can taste the flavours of cheesecake in the custard but texturally it is (and is intended to be) entirely different.

1 × baked Shortcrust Pastry shell (page 23)
70 g (2½ oz) Dulce de Leche (page 139)

Blackberry gel
200 g (7 oz) blackberries
80 g (2¾ oz) water
110 g (4 oz) caster (superfine) sugar
5 g (0.2 oz) pectin NH
5 g (0.2 oz) citric acid

Cheesecake custard
215 g (7½ oz) cream cheese
390 g (14 oz) pouring (whipping) cream
5 g (0.2 oz) orange zest
135 g (5 oz) caster (superfine) sugar
260 g (9 oz) egg yolk

Preheat the oven to 125°C (255°F).

Blackberry gel
Put the blackberries into a narrow measuring jug or container and use a hand-held blender to blend until very smooth. Put the blackberry puree and water into a saucepan and bring to the boil. Combine the sugar with the pectin and add to the blackberry puree, whisk this mixture in and bring to the boil again. Remove from heat. Add the citric acid and use a hand-held blender to blend until smooth, then pass through a fine sieve. Transfer the gel to the fridge to cool and set until firm.

Cheesecake custard
Gently microwave the cream cheese briefly until softened. Add the cream, orange zest and sugar to a saucepan and bring to a simmer over medium heat, then remove from heat immediately. To temper the egg yolks, add them to a mixing bowl and whisk in a small amount of the hot cream mixture until well incorporated. Then add the remaining cream mix and cream cheese and use a hand-held blender to blend until the mixture is shiny and smooth – to prevent any air from being incorporated into the mix, keep the head of the blender underneath the surface. Strain the mixture through a sieve into a measuring jug to use straight away – you want to keep it as warm as possible to ensure it cooks evenly in the oven.

To assemble and bake
Spread the dulce de leche over the base of the prepared pastry shell and place in the oven. Pour the custard on top of the caramel layer. Bake for 30 minutes, or until the custard is slightly wobbly in the centre, then remove from the oven and allow to cool.

To glaze
Once the custard has cooled sufficiently, melt the blackberry gel in a small saucepan over a low heat (you can pop the tart into the fridge to help the custard to firm up, this will also help the gel to set faster). Then, once the gel has fully melted and has started to simmer slightly, pour 220 g (8 oz) of the gel in a circular motion from the inside of the tart and moving outwards. Gently transfer the tart to the fridge to allow to set.

Once the gel is firm to the touch, remove the tart from the tin and portion into slices (see page 39) with a hot, sharp knife.

Raspberry and Jasmine Cheesecake Tart

The inspiration for this tart came from a dessert Gareth used to make at Dinner by Heston Blumenthal in London. Roasted white peaches were macerated in jasmine syrup and plated with yoghurt cream, freeze-dried raspberries and a raspberry meringue, served alongside a cold-infused jasmine tea. Raspberry and jasmine are such an impactful flavour combination. A cheesecake custard with jasmine works perfectly as the high fat and dairy content softens the tannins in the tea and makes its fragrance the real hero.

1 × baked Shortcrust Pastry shell (page 23)
70 g (2½ oz) Dulce de Leche (page 139)

Raspberry gel
200 g (7 oz) raspberries
80 g (2¾ oz) water
110 g (4 oz) caster (superfine) sugar
5 g (0.2 oz) pectin NH

5 g (0.2 oz) citric acid

Cheesecake custard
200 g (7 oz) cream cheese
360 g (12½ oz) pouring (whipping) cream
10 g (¼ oz) jasmine tea
125 g (4½ oz) caster (superfine) sugar
240 g (8½ oz) egg yolk

Preheat the oven to 125°C (255°F).

Raspberry gel
Put the raspberries into a narrow measuring jug or container and blend with a hand-held blender until very smooth. Place a saucepan with the raspberry puree and water on the stove and bring to the boil. Combine the sugar with the pectin then add to the liquid and whisk this mixture in and boil again. Remove from heat, add the citric acid, and use a hand-held blender to blend until smooth, then pass through a fine sieve. Allow the gel to cool and set until firm.

Cheesecake custard
Gently microwave the cream cheese briefly to soften. Add the cream, jasmine tea and sugar to a saucepan and bring to a simmer over medium heat, then remove from heat immediately. To temper the egg yolks, add them to a mixing bowl and whisk in a small amount of the hot cream mixture until well incorporated. Then add the remaining cream mix and cream cheese and use a hand-held blender to blend until the mixture is shiny and smooth – to prevent any air from being incorporated into the mix, keep the head of the blender underneath the surface.

Strain the mixture through a sieve into a measuring jug to use straight away – you want to keep it as warm as possible to ensure it cooks evenly in the oven.

To bake
Spread the dulce de leche over the base of the prepared pastry shell and place in the oven. Pour the custard on top of the caramel layer. Bake for 30 minutes, or until the custard is slightly wobbly in the centre, then remove from the oven and allow to cool.

To glaze
Once the custard has cooled sufficiently, melt the raspberry gel in a small saucepan over a low heat (you can pop the tart into the fridge to help the custard to firm up, which will also help the gel set faster). Then, once the gel has fully melted and has started to simmer slightly, pour 220 g (8 oz) of the gel in a circular motion from the inside of the tart and moving outwards. Gently transfer the tart to the fridge to allow to set.

Once the gel is firm to the touch, remove the tart from the tin and portion into slices with a hot, sharp knife (see page 39).

Mango and Macadamia Tart

If you didn't think that the Mango Weis Bar was the epitome of hot summers growing up then you probably didn't grow up in Australia (apologies for alienating any international readers). Mango and macadamia is a cracking flavour combination, sure, but this tart (and the Weis Bar) is all about the perfectly harmonious marriage of fruity and creamy. Macadamias are expensive, but please don't skimp and use a different nut, we guarantee there is no substitute. It's also worth pointing out that this tart is absolutely brilliant eaten frozen, as we found out after a rather forgetful chef recovered one from the depths of the blast chiller one hot December morning.

1 × baked Shortcrust Pastry shell (page 23)
70 g (2½ oz) Dulce de Leche (page 139)

Macadamia cream glaze
200 g (7 oz) macadamia nuts
700 g (1 lb 9 oz) milk
300 g (10½ oz) cream
100 g (3½ oz) caster (superfine) sugar
3 g salt (0.1 oz)
12 g (0.4 oz) pectin X58

Mango custard
2 ripe mangoes
    (to yield 255 g/9 oz mango puree)
100 g (3½ oz) pouring (whipping) cream
150 g (5½ oz) double (heavy) cream
150 g (5½ oz) caster (superfine) sugar
2 g citric acid
90 g (3 oz) egg
220 g (8 oz) egg yolk

Preheat the oven to 125°C (255°F). Spread the dulce de leche over the base of the prepared pastry shell.

Macadamia cream glaze
Roast the macadamias until they are a light golden brown. Place these into a saucepan with the milk and cream. Bring to a simmer over medium heat, then remove from heat. Break up the macadamias in the mixture with a hand-held blender to maximise the surface area and improve the flavour extraction. Cover, then allow to infuse for half an hour.

Pass the blended macadamia mixture though a fine sieve. Measure 800 g (1 lb 12 oz) of the strained liquid into a saucepan and bring to a boil. Mix the sugar and salt together with the pectin, then rain this mixture into the boiling cream. Return to the boil then simmer for 20 seconds, then remove from heat and blend quickly with a hand-held blender, before decanting the glaze into a container to set.

Mango custard
Remove the skin and stone from the mango and chop the fruit into small pieces. Put the mango into a narrow measuring jug or container and blend with a hand-held blender until it becomes very smooth – this really affects how well the custard emulsifies.

Add the mango puree, creams, sugar and citric acid to a saucepan and bring to a simmer over medium heat. Once simmering, remove from heat immediately. To temper the whole eggs and egg yolks, add them to a mixing bowl and whisk in a small amount of the hot cream mixture until well incorporated. Add the remaining cream mixture and use a hand-held blender to blend until the mixture is shiny and smooth – to prevent any air from being incorporated into the mix, keep the head of the blender underneath the surface. Strain the custard into a measuring jug to use straight away – you want to keep it as warm as possible to ensure it cooks evenly in the oven. Pour the custard into the pastry shell, leaving 5 mm (approx. ¼ in) of pastry free at the top for the macadamia cream. →

To bake

Bake for 30 minutes, or until the custard is slightly wobbly in the centre, then remove from the oven and allow to cool. Place the tart in the fridge to help the custard set.

To glaze

Once the tart has cooled, it's ready to be glazed (see page 37). Warm 180 g (6½ oz) of the glaze in a small saucepan over low heat until just melted. Place 150 g (5½ oz) of the remaining glaze in a jug, then blend the two together until smooth and glossy, but still a little runny. (You can return a bit of the mixture back to a saucepan to make sure that the consistency is right before blending together again).

Pour the glaze in a circular motion on top of the mango custard to ensure that the surface is not damaged. Give the tart tin a little swirl and a tap to get the glaze into all the knuckles, then pop in the fridge to cool until the glaze is nicely set.

Once the glaze has completely cooled, remove the tart from the tin and portion into slices (see page 39). Or, put it in the freezer.

Lamington Tart

Gareth's not particularly fond of lamingtons in their 'classic' format, but having the lamington inside the pastry shell allows you to rejig the ratios and place more of an emphasis on the good stuff – more creamy fillings and just enough sponge. We've also put some actual fruit into the jam to make it taste like raspberries. And here's a controversial opinion: the pastry adds a textural 'biscuity' element that perhaps the lamington was missing all along.

1 × baked Shortcrust Pastry shell (page 23)
shredded coconut, for dusting

Raspberry jam
500 g (1 lb 2 oz) raspberries
250 g (9 oz) caster (superfine) sugar,
    plus 150 g (5½ oz)
10 g (¼ oz) pectin jaune
7 g (¼ oz) citric acid
20 g (¾ oz) water

Coconut soak
180 g (6½ oz) coconut milk
25 g (1 oz) caster (superfine) sugar

Vanilla sponge
80 g (2¾ oz) unsalted butter
20 g (¾ oz) milk
2 g salt

2 g vanilla paste, or the seeds from 1 vanilla pod
140 g (5 oz) plain (all-purpose) flour
3 g (0.1 oz) baking powder
150 g (5½ oz) egg
130 g (4½ oz) caster (superfine) sugar

Coconut glaze
125 g (4½ oz) caster (superfine) sugar
12 g (0.4 oz) pectin X58
500 g (1 lb 2 oz) pouring (whipping) cream
500 g (1 lb 2 oz) coconut cream

Chocolate glaze
50 g (1¾ oz) cocoa powder
7 g (¼ oz) pectin X58
2 g salt
90 g (3 oz) caster (superfine) sugar
175 g (6 oz) pouring (whipping) cream
150 g (5½ oz) milk

Preheat the oven to 165°C (330°F).

Raspberry puree
Put the raspberries in a narrow measuring jug or container and blend with a hand-held blender until very smooth. Add the puree to a saucepan and mix with 250 g (9 oz) of the sugar. Allow the mixture to come to the boil while whisking – it will tend to stick to the bottom of the pan. Take the remaining sugar and mix with the pectin. Rain this into the boiling raspberry mixture and continue to cook until it reaches 106°C (223°F), or until the bubbles grow larger and the mixture has thickened. Once the jam is at the right consistency, mix the citric acid with the water until the granules have fully dissolved. Add this to the jam and return to the boil. Pour the jam into a container and allow to set. Spread 120 g (4½ oz) of the raspberry jam over the base of the pastry shell.

Coconut soak
Bring the coconut milk and the sugar to a boil and set aside.

Vanilla sponge
Melt the butter in a saucepan along with the milk, salt and vanilla. Combine all the dry ingredients except for the sugar and pass through a fine sieve into a bowl. Add the eggs and sugar to the bowl of a stand mixer fitted with a whisk attachment. Beat the eggs on high speed until they are pale and fluffy, then slowly but steadily pour the butter mixture into the eggs, ensuring it is being emulsified into the egg mixture. →

Once the butter is fully incorporated, turn off the machine and add the dry ingredients in one go, then increase the speed to high to work them into the egg mix as quickly as possible, ensuring that the flour isn't being over worked or too much air is lost. Pour the sponge mixture directly into the prepared pastry shell. Place in the oven to bake for 25 minutes, or until the centre of the sponge springs back when pressed gently. Remove from the oven. Use a pastry docker or a fork to poke small holes in the cake while still warm. Pour 220 g (8 oz) of coconut soak mix all over the top to ensure that the whole cake has absorbed the liquid. Set aside to cool.

Coconut glaze

Weigh the sugar and pectin in a bowl. Add the cream and coconut cream to a saucepan. Bring the to a boil over medium–high heat, then add the pectin and sugar and keep at a simmer, whisking continuously, for 20 seconds. Blend with a hand-held blender until smooth and glossy, then decant into a container to allow to set before using.

Chocolate glaze

Weigh the cocoa powder, pectin, salt and sugar in a bowl. Add the cream and milk to a saucepan. Bring to a boil over medium–high heat, then add the pectin mixture and keep at a simmer, whisking continuously, for 20 seconds. Blend with a hand-held until smooth and glossy, then decant into a container to allow to set before using.

To glaze

Once the tart has cooled, it's ready to be glazed (see page 34). Warm 160 g (5½ oz) of the coconut glaze in a saucepan until just melted. Pour this mixture over 160 g of cold glaze and mix with a hand-held blender until it is smooth and reaches the texture of a thick custard. Pour this over the baked cake layer and tilt the tart so that the glaze spreads to the edges (to get a smooth and clean look, avoid using a spatula for this). Tap the tart gently on the bench so that the glaze settles evenly and place in the fridge for 5–10 minutes to firm up.

Melt the chocolate glaze in a saucepan over medium–low heat until liquid. Make sure to swirl it around to ensure it is fully melted and no skin has started to form. Remove from heat and very gently pour the glaze over the tart in a circular motion, ensuring that the glaze isn't damaging the coconut layer underneath. Using the same method of tilting and tapping, get the glaze into all the knuckles of the crust, then place in the fridge for a few minutes to set.

Once the glaze is nice and firm, remove the tart from the tin. Cut the tart into portions with a hot, sharp knife (see page 39) and finish with a very sparse sprinkling of shredded coconut over the top.

Espresso Caramel Chocolate Tart

Gareth's relationship with coffee is what many people would describe as pretty unhealthy. The fuel that got him through many years of late nights and early starts in the kitchen, it lumps him in with pretty much every other stereotypical hospitality worker (thankfully, he ditched the cigarettes a decade ago). As a proper addict, he hated seeing the excess shots from our coffee service in the shop going to waste, so, naturally, he needed to come up with a coffee-based tart. This is the result. The flavour combination mirrors the tasting notes from the coffee beans we use at our cafe: caramel, chocolate and almond. This tart is bold on the coffee flavour (just the way we like it) and would make the perfect after-dinner dessert alongside pretty much any type of nightcap you can think of.

1 × baked Shortcrust Pastry shell (page 23)

Espresso caramel
40 g (1½ oz) pouring (whipping) cream
80 g (2¾ oz) espresso (approx. 3 double shots)
280 g (10 oz) caster (superfine) sugar
160 g (5½ oz) milk
16 g (½ oz) salt
130 g (4½ oz) butter
approx. 100 g (3½ oz) Dulce de Leche
    (page 139), see method

Espresso caramel glaze
130 g (4½ oz) espresso (approx. 5 double shots)
480 g (1 lb 1 oz) pouring (whipping) cream

160 g (5½ oz) caster (superfine) sugar,
    plus another 30 g (1 oz) to mix
    with the pectin
80 g (2¾ oz) butter
5 g (0.2 oz) salt
10 g (¼ oz) pectin X58

Chocolate cake batter
90 g (3 oz) plain (all-purpose) flour
140 g (5 oz) natural almond meal
20 g (¾ oz) cocoa powder
3 g (0.1 oz) baking powder
2 g salt
185 g (6½ oz) caster (superfine) sugar
160 g (5½ oz) egg
155 g (5½ oz) Brown butter (page 111)

Preheat the oven to 165°C (330°F).

Espresso caramel
Slightly warm the cream and espresso in a saucepan over medium heat and set aside. Add the sugar, milk, salt and butter to a pan and bring to a gentle simmer. Continue to cook while whisking to ensure it doesn't burn, and reduce the liquid until the mixture becomes thick and caramelised. At this point, remove the caramel from the stove and add the cream and coffee, and whisk to combine. Give it a quick blitz with a hand-held blender until shiny, then allow to cool. Once set, weigh the espresso caramel and mix with an equal weight of dulce de leche and store in a container.

Espresso caramel glaze
Mix the espresso and cream together in a measuring jug and set aside. Add the 160 g (5½ oz) of sugar and a splash of water to a saucepan and bring to a simmer over medium heat. Continue to cook until all the water has evaporated and the sugar begins to caramelise. Once the caramel is a nice and even medium golden brown, add the butter and salt and whisk together until emulsified. Add the espresso-cream mixture to the caramel in three stages, ensuring that the sugar doesn't set and is completely dissolved before each addition. →

Mix the pectin and the 30 g (1 oz) sugar together and add to the caramel cream once it has boiled, then return to a boil whilst whisking. Let it simmer for 20 seconds then blend with a hand-held blender until smooth and glossy. Decant into a container and allow to set before using.

Chocolate cake batter

Weigh the dry ingredients, except the sugar, in a bowl and stir them together. Add the eggs and sugar to a separate mixing bowl. Either with a whisk or a stand mixer fitted with a whisk attachment, slowly combine until the sugar has dissolved. You do not want to incorporate any air at this stage, as it tends to separate when the butter is added and forms a foamy crust, so keep the speed low.

Melt the brown butter in a saucepan. You want this to be warm enough so that the liquid doesn't cool down too quickly, but cool enough so that it doesn't develop any burnt characteristics. If the butter is too hot, it can also fry the egg mixture as you add it, so a thermometer is useful (we aim for roughly 100°C/210°F).

Once the butter comes up to temperature, slowly pour it into the egg and sugar mixture (or add little by little, if whisking by hand). Ensure that the mixture is well emulsified, as this will prevent the butter from bleeding out later, giving the cake a greasy texture. Finally, mix in the dry ingredients, making sure that there are no lumps suspended throughout the batter.

To bake

Spread 200 g (7 oz) of the espresso caramel over the base of the baked pastry shell, then pour 550 g (1 lb 3 oz) of batter on top. Place the tart into the oven to bake for approximately 30 minutes, or until the crust is an even colour and the centre of the tart is firm. Remove from the oven and allow to cool inside the tin.

To glaze

Once the tart has cooled, it's ready to be glazed (see page 34). Gently warm 120 g (4½ oz) of the espresso caramel glaze in a saucepan until just melted. Pour this mixture over 120 g of cold glaze and mix with a hand-held blender until smooth and the texture of thick custard. Pour this over the baked cake and tilt the tart so that the glaze spreads to the edges (for a smooth and clean look here, avoid using a spatula). Tap the tart gently on the bench so that it settles in the corners, and place in the fridge for 5–10 minutes to firm up.

Once the glaze is nice and firm, remove the tart from the tin and portion into slices with a hot, sharp knife (see page 39).

Coconut Pandan Tart

The first time Gareth encountered pandan it was described to him as 'Thai vanilla'. In retrospect, we're not sure how true that is. As a chef Gareth had used it many times to simply make things green, but when we moved to Victoria Street in Richmond (where Vietnamese culture permeates the grocery shops, restaurants and local community), he quickly found that this was the last thing it should be used for. True pandan die-hards have said that this tart needs more pandan flavour, but we made it to be just as much about the coconut and caramel as it is about the pandan. Generally, the reaction to this tart is that it's undeniably delicious and it has quickly became one of the most popular on the menu. You can source pandan from most Asian grocers. The pandan infusion needs 12 hours to infuse, so complete this step ahead of time.

1 × baked Shortcrust Pastry shell (page 23)

Pandan infusion
15 g (½ oz) pandan leaf
150 g (5½ oz) coconut cream
200 g (7 oz) pouring (whipping) cream

Pandan glaze
100 g (3½ oz) caster (supertine) sugar
4 g (0.14 oz) pectin X58
330 g (11½ oz) Pandan infusion, see above

Coconut caramel
120 g (4½ oz) coconut cream
280 g (10 oz) caster (superfine) sugar

16 g (½ oz) salt
160 g (5½ oz) milk
130 g (4½ oz) butter
approx. 100 g (3½ oz) Dulce de Leche
    (page 139), see method

Coconut batter
45 g (1½ oz) plain (all-purpose) flour
60 g (2 oz) natural almond meal
70 g (2½ oz) desiccated (shredded) coconut
2 g baking powder
2 g salt
165 g (6 oz) caster (superfine) sugar
145 g (5 oz) egg
170 g (6 oz) Brown butter (page 111)

Pandan infusion
Cut the pandan leaf into approx. 1 cm (½ in) thick pieces, place into a saucepan with the creams and bring to a simmer over medium heat. Once simmering, remove from heat. Using a hand-held blender, blend until the liquid becomes light green in colour. Allow to cool and leave to infuse overnight.

Pandan glaze
Weigh the sugar and pectin into a bowl. Pour the pandan infusion into a saucepan and warm gently. Remove from heat. Place another saucepan on top of a set of scales and pass the infusion into it through a fine sieve, weighing out the required 330 g (11½ oz). Bring the measured amount to the boil, then add the pectin and sugar mixture and bring back to a boil. Remove from the heat and blend the mixture with a hand-held

blender until smooth. Decant the mixture into a container and cover with plastic to prevent a skin from forming. Cool in the fridge.

Coconut caramel
In a saucepan, bring the coconut cream to a simmer then set aside. Add the sugar, salt, milk and butter to another saucepan and bring to a simmer over medium heat. Continue to cook while whisking, to ensure it doesn't burn, and reduce the liquid until the mixture becomes thick and caramelised. At this point, remove the caramel from the stove, add the coconut cream and whisk to combine. Give it a quick blitz with a hand-held blender until shiny, then allow to cool. Once set, weigh the mixture and mix with an equal weight of dulce de leche and store in a container. →

Coconut batter

Weigh the dry ingredients, except the sugar, in a bowl and stir them together. Add the eggs and sugar to a separate mixing bowl. Either with a whisk or a stand mixer fitted with a whisk attachment, slowly combine until the sugar has dissolved. You do not want to incorporate any air at this stage, as it tends to separate when the butter is added and forms a foamy crust, so keep the speed low.

Melt the brown butter in a saucepan. You want this to be warm enough so that the liquid doesn't cool down too quickly, but cool enough so that it doesn't develop any burnt characteristics. If the butter is too hot, it can also fry the egg mixture as you add it, so a thermometer is useful (we aim for roughly 100°C/210°F).

Once the butter comes up to temperature, slowly pour it into the egg and sugar mixture (or add little by little, if whisking by hand). Ensure that the mixture is well emulsified, as this will prevent the butter from bleeding out later, giving the cake a greasy texture. Finally, mix in the dry ingredients, making sure that there are no lumps suspended throughout the batter.

To assemble and bake

To bake the tart, spread 150 g (5½ oz) of the coconut caramel over the base of the pastry shell, then pour the batter on top. Place the tart into the oven to bake for approximately 30 minutes, or until the crust is an even colour and the centre of the tart is firm. Remove from the oven and allow to cool inside the tin.

Once the tart has cooled, it's ready to be glazed (see page 34). Warm 150 g (5½ oz) of the pandan glaze in a saucepan until just melted. Pour this mixture over 150 g (5½ oz) of cold glaze and mix with a hand-held blender until smooth and the texture of thick custard. Pour this over the baked cake layer and tilt the tart so that the glaze spreads to the edges (for a smooth and clean look, avoid using a spatula). Tap the tart gently on the bench so the glaze settles evenly. Place in the fridge for 5–10 minutes to firm up.

Once the glaze is nice and firm, remove the tart from the tin and portion into slices with a hot, sharp knife (see page 39).

Matcha, Strawberry and Rice Cream Tart

This tart marks the first time we delved into piping creams on top of our creations. Gareth had been resisting this as he always wanted the perfection of something like a baked custard to speak for itself. However, after shooting the TV show *Dessert Masters* in 2023, he was reinvigorated by a newfound love of classic French patisserie, and piping techniques were one of the skills he felt hadn't yet really been explored at Tarts Anon. Here, we use a 'St Honoré' nozzle (pastry tip) for the piping – if you're a visual learner, there are plenty of demos online that will show you the technique.

1 × baked Shortcrust Pastry shell (page 23)
60 g (2 oz) Dulce de Leche (page 139)

Strawberry gel
200 g (7 oz) strawberries
80 g (2¾ oz) water
110 g (4 oz) caster (superfine) sugar
5 g (0.2 oz) pectin NH
5 g (0.2 oz) citric acid

Rice cream
90 g (3 oz) short-grain rice
150 g (5½ oz) water

2 g gold leaf gelatine
225 g (8 oz) milk
50 g (1¾ oz) caster (superfine) sugar
240 g (8½ oz) pouring (whipping) cream

Matcha custard
40 g (1½ oz) double (heavy) cream
450 g (1 lb) pouring (whipping) cream
10 g (¼ oz) matcha powder, plus extra for dusting
130 g (4½ oz) caster (superfine) sugar
55 g (2 oz) white chocolate callets or buttons
180 g (6½ oz) egg yolks

Preheat the oven to 125°C (255°F)

Strawberry gel
Put the strawberries in a narrow measuring jug or container, and blend with a hand-held blender until very smooth. Add the water and strawberry puree to a saucepan and bring to the boil. Combine the sugar with the pectin, then whisk into the puree and bring to the boil again. Remove from heat and add the citric acid. Blend until smooth, then pass through a fine sieve. Allow the gel to cool and set until firm.

Rice cream
To cook the rice, put the rice and the water into a pot and bring to a simmer over medium–high heat. Place a lid on top of the pot, turn the heat down and cook for 15 minutes. Remove from the heat and allow to rest for a further 5 minutes. Bloom the gelatine in iced water. Take 60 g (2 oz) of the cooked rice and add to a pot with

the milk and sugar, then bring to a boil. Remove from heat and use a hand-held blender to blend until thick and smooth. Return the pot to the heat and simmer again, while whisking, to prevent the mixture from sticking to the bottom of the pot. Add the gelatine to the rice puree and mix to combine. Allow to cool and set fully.

Once cool, add the rice puree and the cream to the bowl of a stand mixer, then whip on medium speed until firm peaks form. Transfer the mixture to a piping (pastry) bag fitted with a St Honoré piping tip, or you can cut a horizontal 1.5 cm (approx. ½ in) opening at the end of the piping bag, then cut off one of the edges at an angle to mimic the shape of the tip. →

Matcha custard

Add the creams, matcha and sugar to a saucepan and bring to a simmer over medium heat. Once simmering, add the white chocolate, whisk to combine and remove from heat. To temper the egg yolks, add them to a mixing bowl and whisk in a small amount of the hot cream mixture until well incorporated. Add the remaining cream mixture and use a hand-held blender to blend the mixture until it is shiny and smooth – to prevent air from being incorporated into the mixture, keep the head of the blender underneath the surface. Strain the mixture into a measuring jug to be used straight away – you want to keep it as warm as possible to ensure it cooks evenly in the oven.

To assemble and bake

Spread the dulce de leche over the base of the pastry shell and place in the oven. Pour the custard on top of this layer. Bake for 30 minutes, or until the custard is slightly wobbly in the centre, then remove from the oven and allow to cool.

Once the custard has cooled sufficiently, melt the strawberry gel in a small saucepan over a low heat (you can pop the tart into the fridge to help the custard to firm up, which will also help the gel to set faster). Once the gel has fully melted and has started to simmer slightly, weigh out 220 g (8 oz) of the gel into a measuring jug and pour onto the tart in a circular motion, starting from the inside of the tart and moving outwards. Gently transfer the tart into the fridge and allow to set.

Once the gel is cool, pipe the rice cream into short peaks that overlap to form a swirled pattern over the whole surface of the tart. Set in the fridge for at least 20 minutes to set. Once the cream is firm to the touch, remove the tart from the tin and portion into slices with a hot, sharp knife (see page 39). To finish, dust with a fine coating of matcha.

Chocolate Malt Tart

The process of malting involves soaking grain, allowing it to sprout, and then roasting it. To extract the sugar, the grain (usually barley) is then is boiled in water until it becomes a thick syrup. The flavour that we primarily associate with malt comes from that dark roasting of the grain, which is the hero flavour of this tart. We use three different versions of 'malt': malt extract in the caramel, brewer's malt in the cake, and finally the barley infusion that you make yourself in the glaze. After all that, you'd hope it didn't end up tasting like Milo for grown-ups, but it kind of does.

1 × baked Shortcrust Pastry shell (page 23)

Barley infusion
60 g (2 oz) pearl barley
300 g (10½ oz) milk

Malt caramel
120 g (4½ oz) pouring (whipping) cream
180 g (6½ oz) caster (superfine) sugar
130 g (4½ oz) butter
60 g (2 oz) malt extract
160 g (5½ oz) milk
16 g (½ oz) salt
125 g (4½ oz) Dulce de Leche (page 139)

Chocolate malt glaze
220 g (8 oz) Barley infusion, above
280 g (10 oz) cream
100 g (3½ oz) liquid malt extract
4 g (0.14 oz) salt
10 g (¼ oz) pectin X58
30 g (1 oz) soft brown sugar
110 g (4 oz) milk chocolate callets or buttons

Chocolate batter
90 g (3 oz) plain (all-purpose) flour
140 g (5 oz) natural almond meal
155 g (5½ oz) Brown butter (page 111)
10 g (¼ oz) malt powder
20 g (¾ oz) cocoa powder
3 g (0.1 oz) baking powder
2 g salt
185 g (6½ oz) caster (superfine) sugar
160 g (5½ oz) egg

Preheat the oven to 165°C (330°F).

Barley infusion
First make the barley infusion. Roast the pearl barley at 180°C (360°F) for 45 minutes, or until very dark. Then place in a saucepan with the milk and bring to a boil. Remove from the heat and leave to infuse for 30 minutes. After 30 minutes has passed, place on the stove to warm again, then pass through a sieve into a container.

Malt caramel
Slightly warm the cream in a saucepan, then set aside. Place the sugar, butter, malt extract, milk and salt and in another saucepan and bring to a gentle simmer. Continue to cook until the mixture reduces and becomes thick and caramelised, whisking continuously to ensure it doesn't burn. Then remove the caramel from the heat and whisk in the cream until combined. Give the mixture a quick blitz with a hand-held blender until shiny, then allow to cool. Weigh out 125 g (4½ oz) of the cooled caramel and mix together with the dulce de leche. Store in a container.

Chocolate malt glaze
Weigh and add 220 g (8 oz) of the barley infusion to a saucepan along with the cream, malt extract and salt. Then, weigh the pectin and the sugar in a separate container and set aside. Bring the cream to a boil over medium heat and then add the pectin mixture. →

Whisk this in, and then continue to simmer, while whisking, for 20 seconds. Remove from heat, add the milk chocolate and blend with a hand-held blender until smooth and glossy. Decant into a container and allow to set before using.

Chocolate batter

Weigh the dry ingredients, except the sugar, in a separate bowl and stir them together. Add the eggs and sugar to a separate mixing bowl. Either with a whisk or a stand mixer fitted with a whisk attachment, slowly combine until the sugar has dissolved. You do not want to incorporate any air at this stage, as it tends to separate when the butter is added and forms a foamy crust, so keep the speed low.

Melt the brown butter in a saucepan. You want this to be warm enough so that the liquid doesn't cool down too quickly, but cool enough so that it doesn't develop any burnt characteristics. If the butter is too hot, it can also fry the egg mixture as you add it, so a thermometer is useful (we aim for roughly 100°C/210°F).

Once the butter comes up to temperature, slowly pour it into the egg and sugar mixture (or add little by little, if whisking by hand). Ensure that the mixture is well emulsified, as this will prevent the butter from bleeding out later, giving the cake a greasy texture. Then mix in the dry ingredients, making sure that there are no lumps suspended throughout the batter.

To assemble and bake

To assemble the tart, spread 200 g (7 oz) of the malt caramel over the base of the pastry shell, then pour 550 g (1 lb 3 oz) of batter on top. Place the tart into the oven to bake for approximately 30 minutes, or until the crust is an even colour and the centre of the tart is firm. Remove from the oven and allow to cool inside the tin.

Once the tart has cooled, it's ready to be glazed (see page 34). Warm 120 g (4½ oz) of the chocolate malt glaze in a saucepan until just melted. Pour this mixture over 120 g (4½ oz) of cold glaze and mix with a hand-held blender until smooth and the texture of a thick custard. Pour this over the baked tart and tilt so that the glaze spreads to the edges (avoid using a spatula for this step to get a smooth and clean look). Tap the tart gently on the bench so that it settles in the knuckles of the crust, and place in the fridge for 5–10 minutes to firm up.

Once the glaze is nice and firm, remove the tart from the tin and portion into slices with a hot, sharp knife (see page 39).

Caramelised Apple Crumble Tart

Apple crumble is one of the holiest of desserts, so the idea to put it into tart form took little convincing. Caramelised apples, apple jam, a spiced cake batter and a crunchy, buttery crumble made with feuilletine flakes (essentially the crunchy bits on the outside of a pancake) make up this delicious wintery tart.

At the shop, we make the crumble by combining the feuilletine with some spare pastry trim from our production kitchen to reduce wastage, but we've used a different technique for the crumble in this recipe so it is better suited to home cooks. You can find feuilletine at most specialty providores. If you can't find it, you could omit it entirely, but we really don't recommend it.

1 × baked Shortcrust Pastry shell (page 23)
icing (confectioners') sugar, for dusting
ground cinnamon, for dusting

Caramelised apples
200 g (7 oz) jazz apples
450 g (1 lb) caster (superfine) sugar
120 g (4½ oz) butter
10 g (¼ oz) salt
120 g (4½ oz) verjuice
350 g (12½ oz) apple juice

Apple jam
250 g (9 oz) jazz apples
70 g (2½ oz) caster (superfine) sugar,
    plus 200 g (7 oz)
3 g (0.1 oz) pectin jaune
4 g (0.14 oz) citric acid
15 g (½ oz) water

Cinnamon cake batter
100 g (3½ oz) natural almond meal
55 g (2 oz) plain (all-purpose) flour
2 g baking powder
2 g salt
2 g cinnamon
60 g (2 oz) caster (superfine) sugar
70 g (2½ oz) soft brown sugar
115 g (4 oz) egg
115 g (4 oz) Brown butter (page 111)

Crumble
60 g (2 oz) butter
150 g (5½ oz) plain (all-purpose) flour
20 g (¾ oz) feuilletine
85 g (3 oz) soft brown sugar
2 g salt

Caramelised apples
Peel and core the apples, then cut them in half. Then, cut the apples into approximately 2 cm (¾ in) thick wedges (aim for about 10 slices per apple).

Take a large saucepan and place it over medium heat. Make a direct caramel by adding just enough of the sugar to cover the bottom of the saucepan and letting it melt until it becomes amber in colour. Once it starts to bubble and all the sugar has dissolved, make another layer with the same amount of sugar and continue until all the sugar has been used up.

Next, add the butter and the salt, and whisk until the butter has fully incorporated. Add the verjuice and the apple juice and bring to a boil. Then drop in all the apples, ensuring not to overcrowd the pan, and return to the boil.

Turn the heat down to a very gentle simmer and let the apples cook gently until all the wedges have started to take on the colour of the caramel but are still raw in the centre. Remove the saucepan from heat and decant the apples and the caramel into a container. Transfer to the fridge to sit until they have cooked through and absorbed the poaching liquid. →

Apple jam

Peel, core then finely chop the apples to speed up the cooking process. Take 70 g (2½ oz) of the sugar and mix with the pectin, then set aside (make sure to mix it thoroughly, as the pectin is likely to form lumps and be ineffective in the jam if not evenly dispersed). Then, make a direct caramel with the remaining sugar in the same manner as the poached apple method on the previous page. Once the caramel is a medium brown shade, add the apples and stir them through the caramel. Turn the heat down and cook until the apples to collapse and release their liquid.

Mix the citric acid with the water and set it aside. Then use a whisk to break the apples up and bring to a boil. Add the pectin mixture and continue to cook until the jam reaches 106°C (223°F) degrees, then add the citric acid solution. Remove from heat, decant into a container once cooled slightly, and transfer to the fridge to set.

Cinnamon cake batter

Weigh the dry ingredients, except the sugars, in a separate bowl and stir them together. Add the eggs and sugars to a separate mixing bowl. Either with a whisk or a stand mixer fitted with a whisk attachment, slowly combine until the sugar has dissolved. You do not want to incorporate any air at this stage, as it tends to separate when the butter is added and forms a foamy crust, so keep the speed low.

Melt the brown butter in a saucepan. You want this to be warm enough so that the liquid doesn't cool down too quickly, but cool enough so that it doesn't develop any burnt characteristics. If the butter is too hot, it can also fry the egg mixture as you add it, so a thermometer is useful (we aim for roughly 100°C/210°F).

Once the butter comes up to temperature, slowly pour it into the egg and sugar mixture (or add little by little, if whisking by hand). Ensure that the mixture is well emulsified, as this will prevent the butter from bleeding out later, giving the cake a greasy texture. Finally, mix in the dry ingredients, making sure that there are no lumps suspended throughout the batter.

Crumble

Melt the butter in a saucepan. Combine all the dry ingredients in a mixing bowl. Slowly add the butter to the dry ingredients and mix until a coarse texture forms. Transfer the crumble to the fridge to chill for approximately 20 minutes, so it's easier to handle later – you want to be able to crumble it up again into nice uniform pebbles. Once this is possible, bake it on a baking paper-lined tray (sheet pan) for 15 minutes at 150°C (300°F). Allow to cool before breaking up into rough (approx. 5 mm/¼ in) pieces.

Increase your oven temperature to 165°C (330°F) to preheat for baking the tart.

To assemble and bake

To assemble the tart, spread 160 g (5½ oz) of apple jam over the base of the pastry shell, and arrange the caramelised apples into three concentric circles, ensuring that there is enough space between them for the batter to come into contact with the jam layer.

Pour the batter over the top of the apples and make sure that all the apple pieces are under the surface. Evenly sprinkle 200 g (7 oz) of crumble over the top of the tart and gently press into the batter.

Place the tart into the oven to bake for approximately 30 minutes, or until the crust is an even golden brown and the centre of the tart is firm. Remove from the oven and allow to cool inside the tin.

Once the cake layer has completely cooled, remove the tart from the tin and portion into slices with a hot, sharp knife (see page 39). To finish, dust with a light coating of icing sugar and a light dusting of cinnamon over the top.

Black Forest Tart

The Black Forest gâteau has a reputation as infamous as the forest it is named after. This fruity, chocolatey wonder has experienced something of a renaissance in recent years, something we attribute in part to Heston Blumenthal's *In Search of Perfection*. In this innovative book, he reimagines dishes we've taken for granted as gastronomic masterpieces. His interpretation of the Black Forest gâteau is still the best dessert Gareth's ever had.

Here is our take. We've taken each element of a classic Black Forest gâteau and attempted to make each component the best version of itself. An emphasis on the cherry flavour and increased acidity brings out the red fruit notes you get in a lot of chocolates, and the kirsch glaze brings well, the kirsch. Gareth created another version of a Black Forest tart on the TV show *Dessert Masters* in 2023 that we later sold in our shop, but this version is a touch more simple and admittedly, just as delicious.

---

1 × baked Shortcrust Pastry shell (page 23)

Poached cherries
1 × 680 g (1½ lb) jar of sour cherries
caster (superfine) sugar, see method
citric acid, see method

Cherry jam
200 g (7 oz) jarred sour cherries
140 g (5 oz) caster (superfine) sugar
4 g (0.14 oz) pectin jaune
3 g (0.1 oz) citric acid
15 g (½ oz) water

Kirsch glaze
3 g (0.1 oz) pectin NH
20 g (¾ oz) caster (superfine) sugar
Poached cherries, in their syrup (see left)
25 g (1 oz) kirsch
2 g citric acid

Chocolate batter
125 g (4½ oz) natural almond meal
20 g (¾ oz) cocoa powder
55 g (2 oz) plain (all-purpose) flour
2 g baking powder
2 g salt
165 g (6 oz) caster (superfine) sugar
145 g (5 oz) egg
140 g (5 oz) Brown butter (page 111)

Poached cherries
Strain the sour cherries from the jar and reserve the liquid. For every 100 g (3½ oz) of reserved liquid, measure 60 g (2 oz) of sugar and 2 g of citric acid. Add these to a saucepan with the cherry liquid, bring to the boil, then set aside to cool (this can also be done with the same quantity of fresh pitted cherries, just replace the cherry liquid with water and poach in the syrup until they are soft). Pour this liquid over the sour cherries and let sit in the syrup for at least 3–4 hours before using.

Cherry jam
Strain the cherries from the jar and reserve the liquid. Place the cherries in a narrow measuring jug and blend with a hand-held blender until the fruit is broken down but not pureed. Mix the sugar with the pectin and set aside. Ensure this is mixed thoroughly, as the pectin is likely to form lumps and be ineffective in the jam if not evenly dispersed. Now place the cherry pulp in a pan and bring to a simmer, then add the sugar and pectin mixture and whisk until fully combined. →

Mix the citric acid with the water and set it aside. Cook the cherries until they reach 106°C (225°F), and the jam has thickened. Add the citric acid solution and return to the boil, then pour into a container to cool.

Kirsch glaze
Combine the pectin and sugar in a small bowl and whisk to combine. Strain the poached cherries and weigh out 200 g (7 oz) of the syrup into a saucepan. Reserve the poached cherries for assembling the tart. Add the kirsch to the cherry liquid, then bring the liquid to the boil and rain in the pectin mixture. Ensure that this is mixed in well and no lumps form, then bring it back to the boil. Add the citric acid while the mixture is boiling, then remove from heat and decant into a container to cool.

Chocolate cake batter
Weigh the dry ingredients, except the sugar, in a bowl and stir them together. Add the eggs and sugar to a separate mixing bowl. Either with a whisk or a stand mixer fitted with a whisk attachment, slowly combine until the sugar has dissolved. You do not want to incorporate any air at this stage, as it tends to separate when the butter is added and forms a foamy crust, so keep the speed low.

Melt the brown butter in a saucepan. You want this to be warm enough so that the liquid doesn't cool down too quickly, but cool enough so that it doesn't develop any burnt characteristics. If the butter is too hot, it can also fry the egg mixture as you add it, so a thermometer is useful (we aim for roughly 100°C/210°F).

Once the butter comes up to temperature, slowly pour it into the egg and sugar mixture (or add little by little, if whisking by hand). Ensure that the mixture is well emulsified, as this will prevent the butter from bleeding out later, giving the cake a greasy texture. Then mix in the dry ingredients, making sure that there are no lumps suspended throughout the batter.

To assemble and bake
To assemble the tart, spread 170 g (6 oz) of the cherry jam across the base of the tart in an even layer, then arrange the reserved poached sour cherries into three concentric circles with 1 cm (½ in) space between each cherry and then cover with the chocolate batter.

Place the tart into the oven to bake for approximately 30 minutes, or until the centre of the tart springs back when pressed. Remove from the oven and allow to cool inside the tin.

Once the cake layer has completely cooled, warm the kirsch glaze in a small saucepan on a low heat until just melted. Using a pastry brush, coat the top of the tart with a generous layer of kirsch glaze. Once it has set, apply a second coat so that the top of the cake has a deep, vibrant cherry red colour. Allow this second coat to cool, then remove the tart from the tin and portion the slices with a hot, sharp knife (see page 39).

Tiramisu Tart

Let's start this recipe with a disclaimer: this is not a tiramisu. This is a tart *inspired* by the flavours of a tiramisu. The whole thing actually came about by mistake; we were trying to bake a cake underneath a custard. Naturally that custard soaked straight through the cake. It wasn't what we were going for, but it tasted delicious and just like a tiramisu. There are two different coffee flavours happening here – the espresso that soaks into the cake and the coffee beans that are infused into the cream. The coffee bean-infused cream came from a Pier recipe Gareth cooked early in his career – it imparts savoury and toasty flavours to the cream, rather than the fruity and acidic forward profiles in espresso. How very un-tiramisu-like.

1 × baked Shortcrust Pastry shell (page 23)
cocoa powder, for dusting

Hazelnut praline
80 g (2¾ oz) hazelnuts
80 g (2¾ oz) caster (superfine) sugar

Hazelnut cake batter
50 g (1¾ oz) hazelnut meal
45 g (1½ oz) plain (all-purpose) flour
2 g salt
2 g baking powder
120 g (4½ oz) golden caster sugar
110 g (4 oz) egg
55 g (2 oz) Brown butter (page 111)

Marsala soak
20 g (¾ oz) Marsala
25 g (1 oz) caster (superfine) sugar
10 g (¼ oz) espresso
80 g (2¾) milk
40 g (1½ oz) egg
60 g (2 oz) Hazelnut praline, see left

Tiramisu custard
240 g (8½ oz) pouring (whipping) cream
8 g (0.3 oz) coffee beans
50 g (1¾ oz) mascarpone
70 g (2½ oz) golden caster sugar
100 g (3½ oz) egg yolk

Preheat the oven to 165°C (330°F).

Hazelnut praline
Roast the hazelnuts on a baking tray (sheet) in the oven for approximately 15 minutes. Once they are a medium golden brown, remove them from the oven and set aside. If your hazelnuts still have skin on them, pour them onto a tea towel (dish towel) while they are still hot, gather the corners together, and roll them around inside the towel to loosen the skins. Then shake the nuts out of the towel to separate them from the skin. Place a pot over a gentle heat and add the sugar. Continue to cook until the caramel becomes deep brown in colour, then add the warm hazelnuts. Stir this together to coat the nuts, then tip onto a tray to cool.

Hazelnut cake batter
Weigh the dry ingredients, except the sugar, in a bowl and stir them together. Add the eggs and sugar to a separate mixing bowl. Either with a whisk or a stand mixer fitted with a whisk attachment, slowly combine until the sugar has dissolved. You do not want to incorporate any air at this stage, as it tends to separate when the butter is added and forms a foamy crust, so keep the speed low.

Melt the brown butter in a saucepan. You want this to be warm enough so that the liquid doesn't cool down too quickly, but cool enough so that it doesn't develop any burnt characteristics. If the butter is too hot, it can also fry the egg mixture as you add it, so a thermometer is useful (we aim for roughly 100°C/210°F). →

Marsala soak

Bring the Marsala, sugar, espresso and milk to a simmer and add the eggs. Blend with a hand-held blender then weigh out and pour 120 g (4½ oz) of the soak over the cake while still warm. Take 60 g (2 oz) of hazelnut praline and spread an even layer over the top of the soaked cake, then set aside while you prepare the custard.

Tiramisu custard

Place the cream, coffee beans, mascarpone and sugar in a saucepan and bring to a simmer, then remove immediately. To temper the egg yolks, add them to a mixing bowl and whisk in a small amount of the hot cream mixture until well incorporated. Add the remaining cream mixture and use a hand-held blender to blend until the mixture is shiny and smooth – to prevent any air from being incorporated into the mix, keep the head of the blender underneath the surface. Strain into a jug to use straight away – you want to keep the custard as warm as possible to ensure the mixture cooks evenly in the oven.

Once the butter comes up to temperature, slowly pour it into the egg and sugar mixture (or add little by little, if whisking by hand). Ensure that the mixture is well emulsified, as this will prevent the butter from bleeding out later, giving the cake a greasy texture. Then mix in the dry ingredients, making sure that there are no lumps suspended throughout the batter.

1st bake

Pour 400 g (14 oz) of batter in the pastry shell. Place the tart into the oven to bake for approximately 15 minutes, or until the crust is an even colour and the centre of the tart is firm. Remove from the oven and allow to cool inside the tin. Use a pastry docker or a fork and poke small holes in the cake while still warm. Leave to cool.

2nd bake

Place the prepared tart into the oven, then pour the custard over top of the praline layer. Bake for 30 minutes, or until the custard just slightly wobbles in the centre, then remove from the oven and allow to cool.

Once the custard has completely cooled, remove the tart from the tin and portion into slices with a hot, sharp knife (see page 39). To finish, dust each slice with fine layer of cocoa powder on top.

Apricot and Desert Lime Tart

We do not doubt you will be tempted to replace the desert limes with regular limes in this recipe because they're much easier to source, but we implore you not to. Desert limes are nothing like regular limes – they have a lot of bitterness, much less edible flesh, are very acidic and require a lot of (worthwhile) encouragement to make them stand out in a meal. They also have a lovely fragrance that makes them quite distinct from regular limes. This tart was a product of a collaboration we did along with some other Melbourne bakeries and Melbourne Bushfood, who grow and supply native Australian ingredients. We use an apricot puree for this tart, but you could also blend up some tinned apricots for this recipe.

1 × baked Shortcrust Pastry shell (page 23)
500 g (1 lb 2 oz) apricots
70 g (2½ oz) Dulce de Leche (page 139)

Desert lime puree and syrup
160g (5½ oz) caster (superfine) sugar
100 g (3½ oz) water
100 g (3½ oz) desert limes

Apricot gel
200 g (7 oz) apricot puree, see method
60 g (2 oz) Desert lime puree, above

100 g (3½ oz) Desert lime syrup, see above
20 g (¾ oz) caster (superfine) sugar
5 g (0.2 oz) pectin NH
3 g (0.1 oz) citric acid

Apricot custard
255 g (9 oz) apricot puree, see method
100 g (3½ oz) pouring (whipping) cream
150 g (5½ oz) double (heavy) cream
200 g (7 oz) caster (superfine) sugar
220 g (8 oz) egg yolk
90 g (3 oz) egg

Preheat the oven to 125°C (255°F). Place the apricots on a baking tray (sheet) and roast in the oven for approximately 15 minutes. Remove the seeds while still warm. Place the apricots in a food processor and blend until very smooth. Set aside for the apricot gel and custard.

Desert lime puree and syrup
In a saucepan, bring the sugar and water to a boil and add the whole desert limes. Return the syrup to a boil and simmer for 5 minutes, then set aside to cool. Strain the desert limes and reserve the syrup. Put the fruit into a tall measuring jug and blend with a hand-held blender until smooth.

Apricot gel
Combine the desert lime puree, the reserved desert lime syrup and the apricot puree in a small saucepan and bring to a boil. Combine the sugar with the pectin and add to the puree mixture once it comes to a boil, whisking continuously until it comes back to boiling point. Whisk in the citric acid, then

remove from heat. Blend the mixture using a hand-held blender, then pass it through a fine sieve. Allow the gel to cool and set until firm.

Apricot custard
Place the apricot puree, both creams and sugar in a saucepan and bring to a simmer, then remove from heat immediately. To temper the whole eggs and egg yolks, add them to a mixing bowl and whisk in a small amount of the hot cream mixture until well incorporated. Add the remaining cream mixture and use a hand-held blender to blend the mixture until it is shiny and smooth – to prevent any air from being incorporated into the mix, keep the head of the blender underneath the surface. Strain the mixture into a measuring jug to use straight away – you want to keep it as warm as possible to ensure it cooks evenly in the oven. →

To assemble and bake

Spread the dulce de leche over the base of the pastry shell and place in the oven. Pour the custard on top of the caramel layer. Bake for 30 minutes, or until the custard is slightly wobbly in the centre, then remove from the oven and allow to cool.

Once the custard has cooled sufficiently, melt the apricot gel in a small saucepan over a low heat (you can pop the tart into the fridge to help the custard to firm up, this will also help the gel to set faster). Once the gel has fully melted and has started to simmer slightly, weigh out 220 g (8 oz) of the gel into a measuring jug. Pour it into the tart in a circular motion, starting from the inside of the tart and moving outwards. Gently transfer the tart into the fridge and allow to set.

Once the gel is firm to the touch, remove the tart from the tin and portion into slices with a hot, sharp knife (see page 39).

Honey and Almond Shortbread Tart

This one is for the crunchy, nutty granola munchers out there, and it holds its own at any time of the day. Crunchy-yet-crumbly almond shortbread under a sour cream and honey custard? Well, despite needing a degree in the art of tart portioning and having to change your oven temperature three times to get this textural wonderland just right, the liquid-resistant shortbread (thanks to Dr Dulce, see page 137) and warming custard top should be ample persuasion to give this one a crack.

40 g (1½ oz) slivered almonds
1 × baked Shortcrust Pastry shell (page 23),
    raw pastry trim reserved
approx. 50 g (1¾ oz) Dulce de Leche (page 139)
roasted almonds, for grating

Pastry glue
50 g raw pastry offcuts
50 g egg (approx. 1)
40 g water

Almond shortbread
70 g (2½ oz) butter
50 g (1¾) caster (superfine) sugar
75 g (2¾ oz) flour
2 g salt

Honey custard
300 g (10½) cream
60 g (2 oz) cream cheese
70 g (2½ oz) sour cream
115 g (4 oz) honey
155 g (5½ oz) egg yolk

Preheat the oven to 165°C (330°F).

Place the slivered almonds on a baking tray (sheet) and toast in the oven for 10 minutes, or until a light golden brown. Set aside and allow to cool.

Pastry glue
Mix the raw trim from the edges of the pastry shell with the egg and water in a small jug. Using a hand-held blender, blend the mixture until smooth and use a pastry brush to apply a thin coat over the base of the pastry shell.

Almond shortbread
Preheat the oven to 150°C (300°F).

Mix the butter and sugar together in a stand mixer until the sugar has dissolved and the butter has softened. Add the flour, salt and the toasted slivered almonds and mix until just combined. Use a palette knife to spread an even layer of the shortbread mixture over the pastry glue layer, then bake in the preheated oven for 15 minutes, or until light golden brown in colour. Allow to cool before spreading a thin layer of dulce de leche on top. This is going to protect the shortbread from absorbing any moisture from the custard and going soggy. →

Honey custard

Preheat the oven to 120°C (250°F).

Add the creams, cream cheese and honey to a saucepan and bring to a simmer over medium heat. Once simmering, remove from heat immediately. To temper the egg yolks, add them to a mixing bowl and whisk in a small amount of the hot cream mixture until well incorporated. Then, add the remaining cream mixture and whisk again until combined. Use a hand-held blender to blend until the mixture is shiny and smooth – to prevent any air from being incorporated into the mix, keep the head of the blender underneath the surface. Decant into a jug to use straight away – you want to keep it as warm as possible to ensure it cooks evenly in the oven.

To bake

Place the prepared tart into the oven, then pour the custard on top of the dulce de leche layer. Bake for 30 minutes, or until the custard is slightly wobbly in the centre, then remove from the oven and allow to cool.

Once the custard has completely cooled, remove the tart from the tin and portion into slices using a hot, sharp knife (see page 39). Finish each slice with a fine grating of roasted almond on top.

Banana and Brown Butter Tart

When Tarts Anon became a bricks and mortar pastry shop, we wanted a tart to bring the breakfast crowds in along with their morning coffee (this was before the savoury tarts were conceived). Everybody knows that banana bread is only worth eating if it's toasted and has a huge (we mean huge) slathering of butter – and this was the inspiration for this tart. The base is a tasty banana cake and the glaze is all brown butter flavour, giving the sensation of melted butter, but without the greasiness. This would be the perfect tart to have alongside your morning coffee or tea. As for your bananas, just like a banana bread, the riper the better.

1 × baked Shortcrust Pastry shell (page 23)

Brown butter
500 g (1 lb 2 oz) unsalted butter

Banana cake batter
2 ripe bananas
90 g (3 oz) egg
90 g (3 oz) caster (superfine) sugar
90 g (3 oz) soft brown sugar
140 g (5 oz) natural almond meal
90 g plain (all-purpose) flour

3 g (0.1 oz) baking powder
2 g ground cinnamon
2 g salt
70 g (2½ oz) Brown butter, left

Brown butter glaze
180 g (6½ oz) Brown butter, left
400 g (14 oz) milk
4 g (0.14 oz) salt
80 g (2¾ oz) soft brown sugar
10 g (¼ oz) pectin X58

Preheat the oven to 165°C (330°F)

Brown butter
Place the butter into a medium saucepan over medium heat. Once completely melted, allow the butter to simmer gently until it begins to foam. Continue to cook, stirring with a whisk on occasion to prevent burning on the bottom of the saucepan. Once the butter starts to expand, small flecks of browned milk solids appear and the fizzing sound of the butter stops, remove it from the heat and allow to cool slightly.

Strain through a fine sieve to remove the milk solids (this is optional, the milk solids won't change the flavour or texture of the tart). Store this in a container in the fridge until needed.

Banana cake batter
Place the banana into a tall measuring jug and blend with a hand-held blender until it is a smooth puree. Weigh 190 g (6½ oz) of the banana puree into a bowl and add to the eggs and sugars. Either with a whisk or a stand mixer fitted with a whisk attachment, slowly combine until the sugar has dissolved. You do not want to incorporate any air at this stage, as it tends to separate when the butter is added and forms a foamy crust, so keep the speed low.

Weigh the remaining dry ingredients in a separate bowl and stir them together. →

111

To bake
Pour the batter into the bottom of your prepared pastry shell. Place the tart into the oven to bake for approximately 30 minutes, or until the crust is an even golden brown and the centre of the tart is firm. Remove from the oven and allow to cool inside the tin.

Brown butter glaze
To make the brown butter glaze, bring the brown butter, milk and salt to a boil in a small saucepan. Mix the sugar and the pectin together in a bowl to ensure that there are no lumps and the pectin is fully dispersed throughout the sugar.

Once the liquid comes to a boil and the butter has melted, add the sugar mix and simmer gently, while whisking, for 20 seconds. Blend this mixture using a hand-held blender and pour into a container to set.

To assemble
Once the tart has cooled, it's ready to be glazed (see page 34). Warm 120 g (4½ oz) of the brown butter glaze in a saucepan until just melted. Pour this mixture over 120 g (4½ oz) of cold glaze and mix with a hand-held blender until smooth and the texture of a thick custard. Pour this over the baked tart and tilt so that the glaze spreads into the edges. (Avoid using a spatula for this step to get a smooth and clean look). Tap the tart gently on the bench so that it settles and place in the fridge for 5–10 minutes to firm up.

Once the glaze is nice and firm, portion the tart into slices with a hot, sharp knife (see page 39).

Melt the brown butter in a saucepan. You want this to be warm enough so that the liquid doesn't cool down too quickly, but cool enough so that it doesn't develop any burnt characteristics. If the butter is too hot, it can also fry the egg mixture as you add it, so a thermometer is useful (we aim for roughly 100°C/210°F). Once the butter comes up to temperature, slowly pour it into the egg, sugar and banana mixture (or add little by little, if whisking by hand). Ensure that the mixture is well emulsified, as this will prevent the butter from bleeding out later, giving the cake a greasy texture. Finally, mix in the dry ingredients, making sure that there are no lumps suspended throughout the batter.

Mango and Yuzu Tart

Yuzu is a magical flavour that pairs perfectly with almost anything. Here we put our best players onto the field and hoped they could get past their egos to create a combination greater than the sum of their parts. This recipe combines yuzu cheesecake custard with a mango glaze and, since we're writing this just as this tart hits the menu for May 2023, we hope our customers have liked it as much as we do (or else this book will be published without pages 114 and 115).

---

1 × baked Shortcrust Pastry shell (page 23)
70 g (2½ oz) Dulce de Leche (page 139)

Mango gel
2 ripe mangoes (to yield 200 g/7 oz mango puree)
140 g (5 oz) water
50 g (1¾ oz) caster (superfine) sugar
5 g (0.2 oz) pectin NH

3 g (0.1 oz) citric acid

Yuzu custard
200 g (7 oz) cream
125 g (4½ oz) caster (superfine) sugar
250 g (9 oz) cream cheese
110 g (4 oz) yuzu juice
250 g (9 oz) egg yolk

Preheat the oven to 125°C (255°F).

Mango gel
Remove the skin and stone from the mango and chop the fruit into small pieces. Put the mango into a narrow measuring jug or container and blend with a hand-held blender until it becomes very smooth – this really affects how well the gel emulsifies.

Add the water and mango puree to a saucepan and bring to the boil. Combine the sugar with the pectin and add to the mango puree and whisk this mixture in and boil again. Add the citric acid, then remove from heat. Use a hand-held blender to blend until smooth, then pass through a fine sieve into a container. Allow the gel to cool and set until firm.

Yuzu custard
Place the cream, sugar, cream cheese and yuzu juice in a saucepan and bring to a simmer, then remove from heat immediately. To temper the egg yolks, add them to a mixing bowl and whisk in a small amount of the hot cream mixture until well incorporated.

Add the remaining mixture and use a hand-held blender to blend until the mixture is shiny and smooth – to prevent any air from being incorporated into the mix, keep the head of the blender underneath the surface. Strain the mixture through a sieve into a measuring jug to use straight away – you want to keep it as warm as possible to ensure the mixture cooks evenly in the oven.

To assemble and bake
Spread the dulce de leche over the base of the pastry shell and place in the oven. Pour the custard on top of the caramel layer. Bake for 30 minutes, or until the custard is slightly wobbly in the centre, then remove from the oven and allow to cool.

Once the custard has cooled sufficiently, melt the mango gel in a small saucepan over a low heat (you can pop the tart into to the fridge to help the custard to firm up, which will also help the gel to set faster). Once the gel has fully melted and has started to simmer slightly, weigh out 220 g (8 oz) of the gel into a measuring jug. Pour it into the tart in a circular motion, starting from the inside of the tart and moving outwards. Gently transfer the tart into the fridge and allow to set.

Once the gel is firm to the touch, remove the tart from the fridge and portion into slices using a hot, sharp knife (see page 39).

Anzac Biscuit Tart

Chewy or crunchy? We tried to settle the debate with this take on an Anzac biscuit by making a tart that is decidedly both: a true celebration of the combination of these textural delights. The biscuit recipe is from the same petit four that inspired the Earl Grey Chocolate and Caraway Tart (page 134), which is the gift that keeps on giving. The recipe calls for you to bake the crispy biscuit separately and place it on top of the chewy coconut and golden syrup cake underneath.

1 × baked Shortcrust Pastry shell (page 23)
icing (confectioners') sugar, for dusting

Coconut caramel
120 g (4½ oz) coconut cream
280 g (10 oz) caster (superfine) sugar
16 g (½ oz) salt
160 g (5½ oz) milk
130 g (4½ oz) butter
approx. 100 g (3½ oz) Dulce de Leche
    (page 139), see method

Anzac biscuit
50 g (1¾ oz) butter
10 g (¼ oz) water
25 g (1 oz) golden syrup

60 g (2 oz) plain (all-purpose) flour
35 g (1¼ oz) quick oats
60 g (2 oz) soft brown sugar
40 g (1½ oz) desiccated (shredded) coconut
1 g salt
2 g bicarbonate of soda (baking soda)

Coconut cake batter
65 g (2¼ oz) natural almond meal
75 g (2¾ oz) desiccated coconut
90 g (3 oz) plain (all purpose) flour
3 g (0.1 oz) baking powder
2 g salt
185 g (6½ oz) caster (superfine) sugar
160 g (5½ oz) egg
155 g (5½ oz) Brown butter (page 111)

Coconut caramel
In a saucepan, bring the coconut cream to a simmer and set aside. Add the sugar, salt, milk and butter to another saucepan bring to gentle simmer over medium heat. Continue to cook while whisking, to ensure it doesn't burn, and reduce the liquid until the mixture becomes thick and caramelised. At this point, remove the caramel from the stove, add the coconut cream and whisk to combine. Give it a quick blitz with a hand-held blender until shiny, then allow to cool. Once set, weigh this mixture and mix with an equal weight of dulce de leche and store in a container.

Anzac biscuit
Preheat your oven to 150°C (300°F).

Place the butter, golden syrup and water in a saucepan and warm gently.

Mix all of the dry ingredients except the bicarbonate of soda in a bowl and set aside. Once the butter and syrup mixture has fully dissolved, bring to a simmer and whisk in the bicarbonate of soda. As soon as the syrup foams and expands, pour into the bowl of dry ingredients and mix well. Once a dough has formed spread it into a circle the same size as the base of your tart tin. Bake this mixture for 15 minutes, then turn the oven down to 120°C (250°F) and bake for a further 10 minutes. Then, while the biscuit is still hot, place the base of the tart tin on top and cut around it to get a clean circle.

Allow this to cool and set aside for later. Increase your oven temperature to 165°C (330°F) to preheat for baking the tart. →

Coconut cake batter

Weigh the dry ingredients, except the sugar, in a bowl and stir them together. Add the eggs and sugar to a separate mixing bowl. Either with a whisk or a stand mixer fitted with a whisk attachment, slowly combine until the sugar has dissolved. You do not want to incorporate any air at this stage, as it tends to separate when the butter is added and forms a foamy crust, so keep the speed low.

Melt the brown butter in a saucepan. You want this to be warm enough so that the liquid doesn't cool down too quickly, but cool enough so that it doesn't develop any burnt characteristics. If the butter is too hot, it can also fry the egg mixture as you add it, so a thermometer is useful (we aim for roughly 100°C/210°F).

Once the butter comes up to temperature, slowly pour it into the egg and sugar mixture (or add little by little, if whisking by hand). Ensure that the mixture is well emulsified, as this will prevent the butter from bleeding out later, giving the cake a greasy texture. Finally, mix in the dry ingredients, making sure that there are no lumps suspended throughout the batter.

To assemble and bake

To assemble the tart, spread 150 g (5½ oz) of the coconut caramel over the base of the tart, then pour 650 g (1 lb 7 oz) of the coconut batter on top. Place the biscuit circle on top, then transfer the tart into the oven to bake for approximately 30 minutes, or until the crust is an even colour and the centre of the tart is firm. Remove from the oven and allow to cool inside the tin.

Once cool, remove the tart from the tin and portion into slices (see page 39). Finish each slice with a dusting of icing sugar.

White Peach and Ume Tart

This tart was initially inspired by one of Gareth's favourite desserts, a dish he made in one of his first jobs at Pier restaurant in Sydney. It was a white peach sorbet with white peaches, mango jelly and a boozy Sauternes-based custard. Many years later, working as a development chef at Lune Croissanterie, he created a pastry using a similar flavour combination for a mini croissant tart, but COVID-19 struck and it never made it to the menu. So you could say this tart was a long time in the making. Umeshu is a sweet, fruit-forward liqueur that is made from Japanese plums (called ume), and pairs perfectly with stone fruits.

1 × baked Shortcrust Pastry shell (page 23)
70 g (2½ oz) Dulce de Leche (page 139)

White peach puree
5 large, ripe white peaches
200 g (7 oz) caster (superfine) sugar
300 g (10½ oz) water
A few sprigs of lemon thyme

White peach gel
200 g (7 oz) White peach puree, above
60 g (2 oz) reserved syrup, see method

80 g (2¾ oz) water
15 g (½ oz) caster (superfine) sugar
5 g (0.2 oz) pectin NH
5 g (0.2 oz) citric acid

Ume custard
550 g (1 lb 3 oz) pouring (whipping) cream
90 g (3 oz) cream cheese
160 g (5½ oz) caster (superfine) sugar
65 g (2¼ oz) umeshu
260 g (9 oz) egg yolk

Preheat the oven to 125°C (255°F).

White peach puree
Cut the peaches in half, discarding the stones, then bring the sugar, water and thyme to a boil. Place the peaches into the syrup and simmer until they are soft. Transfer the fruit pieces to a blender and blend in until smooth. Pass the syrup through a fine sieve and reserve 60 g (2 oz) of the syrup for the gel.

White peach gel
Add the peach puree, reserved syrup and water to a saucepan and bring to the boil. Combine the sugar with the pectin and whisk this mixture in while bringing back to the boil. Add the citric acid and remove from heat. Use a hand-held blender to blend until smooth, then pass the mixture through a fine sieve. Allow the gel to cool and set until firm.

Ume custard
Place the cream, cream cheese, sugar and umeshu in a saucepan and bring to a simmer, then immediately remove from heat. To temper the egg yolks, add them to a mixing bowl and whisk in a small amount of the hot cream mixture until well incorporated. Add the remaining cream mixture and use a hand-held blender to blend until the mixture is shiny and smooth – to prevent any air from being incorporated into the mix, keep the head of the blender underneath the surface. Strain the mixture through a sieve into a measuring jug to use straight away – you want to keep it as warm as possible to ensure the mixture cooks evenly in the oven. →

To bake

Spread the dulce de leche over the base of the prepared pastry shell and place in the oven. Pour the custard on top of the caramel layer. Bake for 30 minutes, or until the custard is slightly wobbly in the centre, then remove from the oven and allow to cool.

To glaze

Once the custard has cooled sufficiently, melt the white peach gel in a small saucepan over a low heat (you can pop the tart into the fridge to help the custard to firm up, which will also help the gel to set faster). Once the gel has fully melted and has started to simmer slightly, weigh out 220 g (8 oz) of the gel into a measuring jug. Pour it into the tart in a circular motion, starting from the inside of the tart and moving outwards. Gently transfer the tart into the fridge and allow to set.

Once the gel is firm to the touch, remove the tart from the tin and portion into slices with a hot sharp knife (see page 39).

Rice Pudding Brûlée Tart

Gareth took issue with Cat calling this a rice pudding brûlée because he says it isn't a rice pudding, but she thought it would sell better this way in the shop (she's a huge rice pudding fan herself) and it turns out she was right, because it was extraordinarily popular. This is inspired by a pastry Gareth used to eat when he was living in Holland and working at the three-Michelin-star restaurant, Oud Sluis. The restaurant sat close to the Belgian border and with it, rijsttaartje – a traditional Flemish pastry – became something he would regularly indulge in. We like to think this tart is a refined homage to that delicious and memorable pastry.

The brûlée is best done right before serving but, because of the starch in the rice, the custard forms a thin skin on the top which slows the dissolving of the toffee – so if you need to let it hang around for a bit, this will buy you that little bit of extra time.

---

1 × baked Shortcrust Pastry shell (page 23)
70 g (2½ oz) Dulce de Leche (page 139)
caster (superfine) sugar, for the brûlée

Rice custard
75 g (2¾ oz) cooked short-grain rice
180 g (6½ oz) milk
580 g (1 lb 4 oz) cream

230 g (8 oz) soft brown sugar
1 g ground cinnamon
3 g (0.1 oz) lemon zest
3 g (0.1 oz) vanilla paste, or the seeds
    from a vanilla pod
250 g (9 oz) egg yolk
3 g (0.1 oz) salt

Preheat the oven to 165°C (330°F).

Rice custard
In a saucepan, combine the cooked rice, milk, cream, sugar, cinnamon, lemon zest and vanilla and bring to a simmer while whisking. Once boiled, transfer to a blender and blitz on high for 2 minutes or until it becomes a smooth puree. Strain through a sieve and pour a small amount onto the egg yolks to temper them. Whisk this together until incorporated, then add the remaining cream mixture and the salt. Using a hand-held blender, blend until the mixture is shiny and smooth – to prevent air from being incorporated into the mix, keep the head of the blender underneath the surface. Decant into a measuring jug to use straight away – you want to keep it as warm as possible to ensure the mixture cooks evenly in the oven.

To assemble and bake
Spread the dulce de leche over the bottom of the pastry shell. Place the tart into the oven and pour the custard on top of the caramel layer. Bake for 30 minutes, or until the custard is slightly wobbly in the centre, then remove from the oven and allow to cool.

Once the custard has completely cooled, remove the tart from the tin. Portion the tart into slices (see page 39) using a hot, sharp knife. Sprinkle each slice with a generous amount of caster sugar. Using a blowtorch, caramelise the sugar until it is deep golden brown in colour and evenly distributed across the tart.

Passionfruit and Ginger Tart

Jams that sit underneath a custard are not for the faint-hearted baker, but they are the cornerstone of many of our tart recipes. Sugar, resplendent in jams, is hygroscopic, meaning that it will absorb any moisture. When you pour a liquid custard on top, that liquid is then absorbed by the jam, making it very watery and thin. This is why it's important to make the jam thick (more like a sweetened fruit paste than a jam) and why we've made this particular jam using crystallised ginger, which is composed mostly of the fibrous tissue of the ginger, instead of infusing ginger into a fruit juice as would be more typical.

1 × baked Shortcrust Pastry shell (page 23)

Ginger jam
120 g (4½ oz) crystallised ginger
80 g (2¾ oz) passionfruit juice
4 g (0.14 oz) citric acid
5 g (0.2 oz) water
30g (1 oz) sugar
2 g pectin jaune

Passionfruit custard
135 g (5 oz) pouring (whipping) cream
190 g (6½ oz) double (heavy) cream
250 g (9 oz) caster (superfine) sugar
180 g (6½ oz) passionfruit juice
105 g (3½ oz) egg
220 g (8 oz) egg yolk

Preheat the oven to 125°C (255°F).

Ginger jam
Cut the crystallised ginger into small pieces and place into a small saucepan along with the passionfruit juice and bring to a gentle simmer – we are just trying to hydrate the ginger to soften it at this point, so be sure not to cook too aggressively. Place this mixture into a measuring jug and use a hand-held blender to blend until it forms a thick paste, then return the mixture the saucepan and bring to the boil. Meanwhile, mix the citric acid with the water in a small bowl and allow to dissolve, then set aside.

In another small bowl, mix the sugar and pectin together and add to the ginger mixture once it returns to the boil. Stir this gently and cook until it becomes a thick paste, then add the citric acid and water solution and stir again. Once the mixture has returned to the boil, remove from heat and pour into a container to set. Be sure to keep this paste at room temperature – if not it will need to be warmed slightly before being added to the pastry shell. Evenly spread 90 g (3 oz) of this mix over the base of the pastry shell.

Passionfruit custard
Place the creams, sugar and passionfruit juice in a saucepan and bring to a simmer, then remove from heat immediately. To temper the whole eggs and egg yolks, add them to a mixing bowl and whisk in a small amount of the hot cream mixture until well incorporated. Add the remaining cream mixture and use a hand-held blender to blend until the mixture is shiny and smooth – to prevent any air from being incorporated into the mix, keep the head of the blender underneath the surface.

Strain the custard into a measuring jug and let sit for 5 minutes for all the impurities to rise to the top, then remove them with a ladle. Once the surface is clear of bubbles, pour the custard into the pastry shell straight away to ensure the mixture cooks evenly in the oven.

To bake
Bake for 30 minutes, or until the custard is slightly wobbly in the centre, then remove from the oven and allow to cool. Once completely cooled, remove the tart from the tin and portion into slices with a hot, sharp knife (see page 39).

Pistachio and Date Tart

We like to think people come to our shop for the Chocolate and Caramel Tart (page 56) and Plain Old Lemon Tart (page 48) but that they stay for the Pistachio and Date Tart. These two bold Middle Eastern flavours pair perfectly together. We hoped that people who had faith in our model would try it and enjoy it like we do. Sure, it's never sold as well as some of our other tarts, but it's one people have always remembered and called for when it left the menu. Whether you make it or not is up to you, but if you do, you will have our ultimate respect forever (and also a delicious tart).

To blend the pistachios, you will need a powerful food processor, but if you don't have one, 100% pistachio paste is available from a lot of specialty ingredient stores.

1 × baked Shortcrust Pastry shell (page 23)
pistachio meal or powder (or raw pistachios, pulsed in a food processor), for dusting

Pistachio paste
300 g (10½ oz) pistachios, shelled, or good quality pistachio paste

Date puree
300 g (10½ oz) fresh dates, or dried dates that have been rehydrated in water

Pistachio custard
550 g (1 lb 3 oz) pouring (whipping) cream
4 g (0.14 oz) salt
130 g (4½ oz) caster (superfine) sugar
230 g (8 oz) egg yolk
90 g (3 oz) Pistachio paste, left
green food colour (optional)
yellow food colour (optional)

Preheat the oven to 120°C (250°F).

Pistachio paste
Toast the pistachios in the oven on a baking tray (sheet) for 45 minutes. Keeping the temperature low for a long period of time will allow the nuts to stay nice and green while removing all of the moisture. Once you've removed the pistachios from the oven, increase the heat to 125°C (255°F) to preheat for baking the tart. When the pistachios have cooled, add them to a food processor and blend until smooth, around 5 minutes.

Date puree
Remove the stones from the dates and place the flesh into a food processor. If you feel as though the dates you're using are a little on the bland side, add a little bit of icing sugar to boost the sweetness. If you've soaked dried dates, make sure they are well drained. They might blend better when they are a little wetter, but the taste will be that much nicer the more intense it is. Once the date puree is smooth, spread 150 g (5½ oz) over the base of the pastry shell. Set this aside while you prepare the custard mix.

Pistachio custard
Place the cream, salt and sugar in a saucepan and bring to a simmer, remove immediately. Next, temper the egg yolks in a mixing bowl by pouring a small amount of the hot cream mixture onto them and whisking the two together until incorporated. Add a small amount of the cream mixture to the pistachio paste and whisk to combine. Add the remaining mixture and the tempered eggs, then using a hand-held blender, blend until the mixture is shiny and smooth – to prevent any air from being incorporated into the mix, keep the head of the blender underneath the surface. At this point, you can add the smallest amount of yellow and green food colour to get a more vibrant pistachio hue as the egg yolk tends to brown the mix somewhat. →

Pass the custard through a fine sieve into a measuring jug to use straight away – you want to keep it as warm as possible to ensure the mixture cooks evenly in the oven.

To bake
Place the pastry shell into the oven, then pour the custard over the date layer. Bake for 30 minutes, or until the custard is slightly wobbly in the centre, then remove from the oven and allow to cool.

Once the custard has completely cooled, remove the tart from the tin and portion into slices using a hot, sharp knife (see page 39). To finish, dust each slice with a light coating of pistachio powder.

Ube and Coconut Tart

One of our sous chefs, the lovely Kitty Budihardjo, suggested making a tart that featured ube (a purple yam native to Southeast Asia), which is popular in Indonesia, where she grew up. Ube is a particularly comforting snack in the colder months due to its warmth and natural sweetness. Ube now comes in various forms (paste, powders), making the flavour easier to incorporate into desserts. We use a combination of purple sweet potato puree and ube extract to achieve the flavours (and bright purple colour) here. Fresh ube is also hard to source in Melbourne, we've found, but you can get the extract from most Asian grocers.

1 × baked Shortcrust Pastry shell (page 23)

Sweet potato purees
200 g (7 oz) purple sweet potato or taro
300 g (10½ oz) orange sweet potato

Ube glaze
60 g (2 oz) caster (superfine) sugar
5 g (0.2 oz) pectin X58
100 g (3½ oz) pouring (whipping) cream
200 g (7 oz) milk
2 g salt
0.5 g ube extract, approx. 10 drops
150 g (5½ oz) Purple sweet potato puree, above

Coconut cake batter
75 g (2¾ oz) natural almond meal
35 g (1¼ oz) desiccated (shredded) coconut
90 g (3 oz) plain (all-purpose) flour
3 g (0.1 oz) baking powder
2 g salt
110 g (4 oz) caster (superfine) sugar
90 g (3 oz) soft brown sugar
65 g (2¼ oz) egg
210 g (7½ oz) Orange sweet potato puree, left
76 g (2¾ oz) Brown butter (page 111)

Preheat the oven to 180°C (360°F).

Sweet potato purees
To make the sweet potato purees, place both the purple and orange sweet potatoes on a rack and poke some holes in them with a fork. Place them in the oven and bake for around 35 minutes, or until they are soft. Allow them to cool slightly before removing the skin and pureeing the purple and orange sweet potatoes separately in a blender. Store both purees in the fridge until ready to use.

Ube glaze
Mix the sugar and the pectin in a small bowl and set aside. Then place the cream, milk, salt and ube extract into a saucepan and bring to a simmer. Once boiled, add the pectin and sugar mixture and return to a boil. Whisk in the purple sweet potato puree and bring to a boil once again. Remove from heat and blend until smooth using a hand-held blender. Decant into a container and cover the surface of the glaze with plastic to prevent a skin from forming. Cool in the fridge.

Coconut cake batter
Weigh the dry ingredients, except the sugar, in a bowl and stir them together. Add the eggs, orange sweet potato puree and sugar to another mixing bowl. Either with a whisk or a stand mixer fitted with a whisk attachment, slowly combine until the sugar has dissolved. You do not want to incorporate any air at this stage, as it tends to separate when the butter is added and forms a foamy crust, so keep the speed low.

Melt the brown butter in a saucepan. You want this to be warm enough so that the liquid doesn't cool down too quickly, but cool enough so that it doesn't develop any burnt characteristics. If the butter is too hot, it can also fry the egg mixture as you add it, so a thermometer is useful (we aim for roughly 100°C/210°F). →

Once the butter comes up to temperature, slowly pour it into the egg and sugar mixture (or add little by little, if whisking by hand). Ensure that the mixture is well emulsified, as this will prevent the butter from bleeding out later, giving the cake a greasy texture. Finally, mix in the dry ingredients, making sure that there are no lumps suspended throughout the batter.

To bake

To bake the tart, pour 650 g (1 lb 7 oz) of batter in the prepared pastry shell. Place the tart into the oven and bake for approximately 30 minutes, or until the crust is an even colour and the centre of the tart is firm. Remove from the oven and allow to cool inside the tin.

To glaze

Once the tart has cooled, it's ready to be glazed (see page 34). Warm 250 g (9 oz) of the ube glaze in a saucepan until just melted. Pour this mixture into a tall measuring jug or container with 150 g (5½ oz) of cold glaze and mix with a hand-held blender until smooth and the texture of thick custard. Pour the glaze over the baked tart and tilt the tin so that the glaze spreads to the edges (for a smooth and clean look, avoid using a spatula). Tap the tart gently on the bench so that it settles into the knuckles of the crust, and place in the fridge for 5–10 minutes to firm up.

Once the glaze is nice and firm, remove the tart from the tin and portion into slices using a hot, sharp knife (see page 39).

Vanilla and Rhubarb Tart

This recipe is a riff on classic Vanilla Custard Tart (page 47) with the addition of a rhubarb compote and rhubarb glaze. It's not that much extra work than a vanilla custard tart, but the reward is tenfold. Before we put this tart on the menu, we ran a vote for our customers asking whether they wanted a 'Vanilla and Rhubarb' or 'Cardamom and Rhubarb' tart and, maybe unsurprisingly, vanilla won. If you're huge cardamom fans like us, simply add 5 g (0.2 oz) of ground cardamom to the custard in place of the vanilla and coffee to make this tart truly fantastic and a bit more unique. You can store the jam (or any jam) in an airtight container in the freezer for pretty much as long as you like – just maybe not until you move house only to open it up and wonder 'What the hell is that?'

1 × baked Shortcrust Pastry shell (page 23)
Vanilla custard (see page 47), warm

Rhubarb compote and syrup
150 g (5½ oz) rhubarb
180 g (6½ oz) caster (superfine) sugar
120 g (4½ oz) water

Rhubarb gel
200 g (7 oz) Rhubarb syrup, see method
50 g (1¾ oz) Rhubarb compote, see left
6 g (0.2 oz) caster (superfine) sugar
6 g (0.2 oz) pectin NH
2 g citric acid

Preheat the oven to 125°C (255°F).

Rhubarb compote and syrup
In a saucepan, bring the rhubarb, sugar and water to the boil, then remove from heat. Once the rhubarb is soft, strain through a sieve and reserve the syrup for the glaze. Set 50 g (1¾ oz) of the rhubarb aside for the gel and spread the remaining rhubarb on a paper-lined tray and place in the oven for about 15 minutes. Once the fruit has dried out slightly into a nice stiff compote, spread 100 g (3½ oz) over the base of the shell.

Rhubarb gel
In a saucepan, bring 200 g (7 oz) syrup and the reserved rhubarb to a simmer. Whisk the sugar and the pectin together and add to the saucepan. Return this mixture to the boil, while whisking, then add the citric acid. Remove from heat, then use a hand-held blender to blend for 1 minute, or until smooth and the rhubarb pieces have broken down. Decant into a container and leave to set in the fridge.

To bake
Place the prepared pastry shell in the oven. Pour the warm vanilla custard over the compote layer. Bake for 30 minutes or until the custard is slightly wobbly in the centre, then remove from the oven and allow to cool.

To glaze
Once the custard has cooled sufficiently, melt the rhubarb gel in a small saucepan over a low heat (you can pop the tart into the fridge to help the custard to firm up, this will also help the gel to set faster). Once the gel has fully melted and has started to simmer slightly, weigh out 220 g (8 oz) of the gel into a measuring jug. Pour it into the tart in a circular motion (see page 37), starting from the inside of the tart and moving outwards. Gently transfer the tart into the fridge and allow to set.

Once the gel is firm to the touch, remove the tart from the tin and portion into slices with a hot, sharp knife (see page 39).

Earl Grey Chocolate and Caraway Tart

During the years that Gareth worked at Dinner By Heston Blumenthal, we were lucky to have many opportunities to dine there together. It was much to Gareth's dismay that Cat's favourite part of the meal was always the very simple (and tiny!) Earl Grey ganache with a caraway biscuit that was served right at the end of the meal, alongside your coffee or tea. It was a no-brainer, then, to recreate this flavour profile in tart form, and this is the result. The flavours here are so delicate and interesting and it's perhaps our favourite of the chocolate tarts in the history of Tarts Anon. Note that you will need to start with a raw pastry shell for this recipe.

1 × raw Shortcrust Pastry shell (page 23)
approx. 50 g (1¾ oz) Dulce de Leche (page 139)
cocoa powder, for dusting

Caraway shortbread
3 g (0.1 oz) caraway seeds
70 g (2½ oz) butter
50 g (1¾ oz) caster (superfine) sugar
75 g (2¾ oz) plain (all-purpose) flour
2 g salt

Chocolate custard
560 g (1 lb 4 oz) pouring (whipping) cream
55 g (2 oz) golden caster sugar
3 g (0.1 oz) salt
5 g (0.2 oz) Earl Grey tea leaves
230 g (8 oz) egg yolk
45 g (1½ oz) dark chocolate (70% cocoa solids) callets or buttons
90 g (3 oz) milk chocolate callets or buttons

Preheat the oven to 165°C (330°F).

Caraway shortbread
Toast the caraway seeds in a saucepan over medium–low heat until fragrant and the seeds start to pop. Set aside and allow to cool.

Mix the butter and sugar together in a stand mixer until the sugar has dissolved and the butter has softened. Add the flour, salt and toasted caraway seeds and mix until just combined. Use a palette knife to spread an even layer of this mixture over the base of the raw pastry shell, then place a circle of baking paper over the top. Place your blind-baking foil and weights on top, then bake for 30 minutes or until light golden brown in colour. Allow this to cool before spreading a thin layer of dulce de leche on top. This is going to protect the shortbread from absorbing any moisture from the custard and going soggy.

Chocolate custard
Add the cream, sugar, salt and tea to a saucepan and bring to a simmer over medium heat. Once simmering, remove from heat immediately. To temper the egg yolks, add them to a mixing bowl and whisk in a small amount of the hot cream mixture until well incorporated. Then, add the remaining cream mixture and whisk again until combined. Add both chocolates and mix until combined. Using a hand-held blender, blend until the mixture is shiny and smooth, keeping the head of the blender underneath the surface. Strain into a jug to remove the tea leaves and use straight away – you want to keep it as warm as possible to ensure it cooks evenly in the oven.

To bake
Place the prepared tart into the oven, then pour the custard on top of the dulce de leche layer. Bake for 30 minutes, or until the custard has a slight wobble in the centre, then remove from the oven and allow to cool.

Once the custard has completely cooled, remove the tart from the tin. Portion into slices with a knife (see page 39) and dust a fine layer of cocoa powder on top.

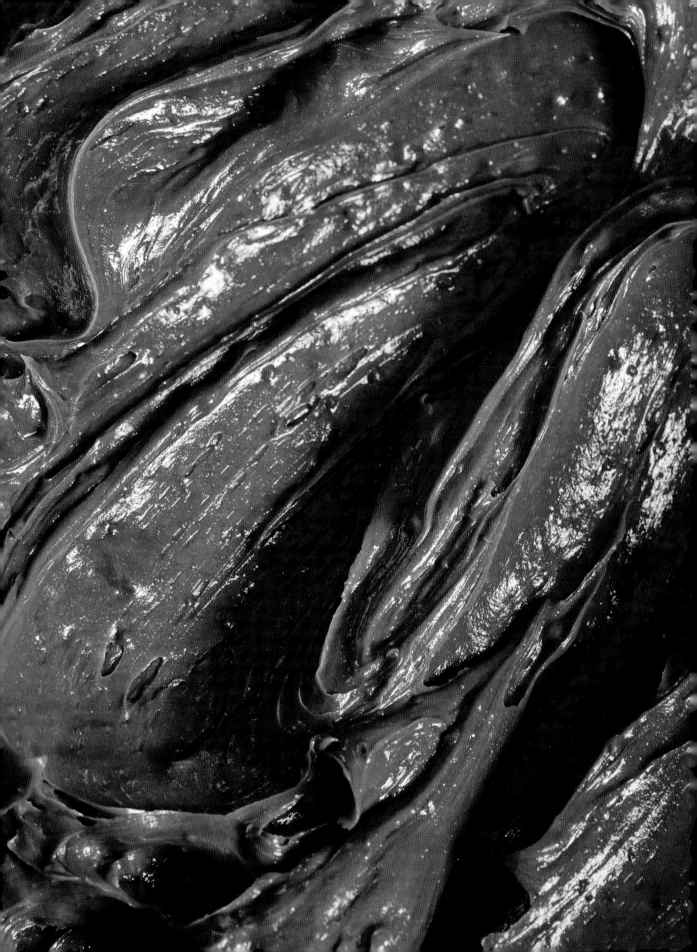

Calling Dr Dulce

Condensed milk, dulce de leche, milk caramel, milk jam – whatever you want to call it, you can almost certainly attribute the success of our business to this humble can. Not only is it delicious enough to earn itself a spot as a major element in our most popular tarts, but it also finds its way into most Tarts Anon recipes in one way or another.

There are many origin stories for dulce de leche. Whether it's the story of a young Argentinian girl who was making a sweet milk drink for her sickly mother, only to be called away from a still lit stove to return to one of the greatest cases of accidental discovery since cheese. Or the exact same story, just replace 'girl' with 'soldiers' and 'sickly mother' with 'bloodshed'. Regardless, this relative of caramel (which for the most part, is superior in almost every way) is made in varying ways at Tarts Anon. One, where we cook sugar and milk together with some other choice ingredients to create sweet, thick milk caramel, but also the more conventional method of throwing cans of condensed milk into a pot of hot water and letting them tick away for hours on end.

Cooking condensed milk cans in boiling water for 6 hours seems like an excellent return on investment considering the abundance of dulce de leche that we go through in the shop. And you'd be right for thinking that, if you then didn't have to open 100 cans, scoop caramel out of them, scrape out the insides and then mix up all of the thick, sticky contents every week on repeat. But despite how tedious and frustrating a job this is, the work involved pales in significance to the final results.

Not all condensed milk is created equal – between the three chief brands available to us when we first started Tarts Anon, we discovered that despite all having the same ingredients and nutritional information, some brands would not thicken in the same way as others. One particular brand would set into an almost gelatinous manner, forming a wobbly caramel cylinder, while the others would become more malleable and manoeuvrable despite the exact same cooking times and conditions. These variables were over analysed to the nth degree; changing the can's position in the pot, simmering vs boiling, differing lengths of time for certain brands vs others, and how they were cooled. For the most part, the results remained consistent, with colour being the only part to change. This is how we worked out which brand we preferred for all applications. Surprisingly it was the cheapest of the lot: Woolworths Homebrand. For reasons not known to us, this humble tin allowed for longer mixing before it started to break down. This is great for when you need to add spices or seasonings to the caramel, and not to mention for cooking it at 165°C (330°F) for over half an hour. If you can't get your hands on the Woolworths brand, we suggest experimenting with the brands you have available to find one that works the best. Remember, the most expensive won't always be the best for this application!

The process, explained

Sugar is a strange ingredient. Its crystal form might make it seem like a malleable, pliant ingredient, but if these small crystals were all to melt and harden back together, you would be left with something as hard as a rock that would break teeth for fun. So, when you make a caramel, you might think that it's the sugar that makes it thicken and set. But in fact, it's the lack of water in a direct caramel that does the trick. And mixing it with dairy fat ensures a smooth caramel that, although thick, won't end up with a texture that would stop bullets.

You might be wondering, 'How does seemingly liquid condensed milk turn into the consistency of old glue when the water has nowhere to go?' You've got a point. In this case, it's the milk proteins and the lactose – not the sucrose from the sugar – that firm up the liquid and turns it a deep, dark brown colour. Much in the same way that a piece of meat cooks (although some of the water is indeed escaping from the meat), the proteins are retracting and forming a structure and caramelising all the while. This process is known as the Maillard reaction, and it's what gives us that deep, nutty, caramelised flavour.

Making dulce de leche this way provides resilience. When mixed, the dulce doesn't lose its structure. When exposed to liquids (and not mixed), it remains solid. When heated, it won't slide away as there's not enough fat for the caramel to lose its viscosity. This also means that it will never split, as the fat content in the condensed milk is remarkably low in comparison to most caramel recipes.

In Dr Dulce we trust

One day Gareth overheard one of our sous chefs refer to the dulce de leche as 'Dr Dulce'. It's a good way to sum up how versatile an ingredient this is. If we ever get a crack in our pastry after it's been baked, we smear a little dulce over it. It will fill the gap and not melt away if you pour your custard inside, and will hold strong up until the custard is set. Custard tarts that get baked fresh every day are susceptible to softening on the base if left to sit for longer than 3–4 hours. A great way to get that 'just baked' freshness out of your tart base? Spread 70 g (2½ oz) of dulce underneath the custard for safety purposes: a process we like to call 'safety dulce'.

Knowing we always have Dr Dulce on call gives us the confidence it has given us to proceed with our pastry recipe and to keep it as thin and as delicate as we have up until now.

P.S. Although eating this stuff by the spoonful will no doubt give you diabetes, there is something so inherently savoury about it. It's probably thanks to the caramelised milk solids that give brown butter that distinctly nutty and savoury flavour, but trust us, as soon as you add salt to your dulce, you'd be forgiven for eating a little bit with your chips … wait.

4   Place the pot onto the stove and bring to a boil, then reduce to a simmer and set a timer for 6 hours. Keep an eye on the water level and top it up with hot water as you go so that the cans stay under water at all times.

The water provides a protective barrier (as it cannot go above 100°C, give or take). Let the water run out, and the milk inside the can will burn on the base as well as expand and explode in some cases. Although the liquid condensed milk is contained inside a can, the parts of the caramel that aren't submerged remain lighter than the parts that are, especially once the proteins start to set and the milk becomes solid.

5   Once the time is up, remove the cans from the water and allow them to cool before opening – trust us. The pressure built up inside the can over time can cause the contents to spit out whilst still hot and it's not a pleasant experience.

You can also leave these cans inside the water until it can be safely removed once the water cools. This may take up to half an hour depending on the amount of cans you've chosen to cook, but the extra bit of time wont change how the caramel comes out.

Dulce de Leche

1   Take any number of 400 g (14 oz) cans of condensed milk and remove the labels. This will make the clean up that much easier and also protect you from any contractual obligation you have to any other canned goods brand.

2   Place the cans lid side up inside a saucepan that will allow you to have at least 2 cm (¾ in) of water above the tops of the cans, but not be in danger of overflowing when the pot boils – roughly another 2 cm (¾ in).

3   Pour hot water into this pot – the hotter the better. This won't affect how the caramel cooks, but the timer starts once the water comes up to temperature, so this just gets you there quicker.

Celebration
Tarts

We believe any tart in this book could reasonably be considered a celebration tart. But if you have an event in mind and can't decide what to bake, then let this section be your guide.

These tarts sit in a separate category because they are made with flavours that are classically associated with certain holidays and celebrations and, for some reason, taste better then, too. Take fruit mince for example. When Gareth said he was going to make an Eggnog and Fruit Mince Tart (page 155), Cat proclaimed, 'I hate fruit mince', to which he confidently responded, 'Yeah, so what, everyone hates fruit mince for 11 months of the year.' There's something about fruit mince, mulled wine, gingerbread, pumpkin, and other flavours you'll find in the tarts in this chapter that make them so much more appealing when it's their time of year to shine. Want some eggnog after dinner in September? No thanks. How about after eating your weight in prawns and turkey on a sweltering Australian Christmas day? Obviously!

There's a huge amount of pressure on desserts that centre around 'occasions' to be incredible. They bring with them a sense of nostalgia: people remember blowing out the candles at their childhood birthday party and tucking into a sickly-sweet cake covered in buttercream and 100s and 1000s sprinkles, the taste of grandma's Christmas pudding; eating toasted hot cross buns with lashings of butter on Easter morning. Take away the emotional connection, and we'd argue that most classic or generic versions of these 'special occasion' treats are just average to a seasoned pastry eater; in many cases the balance is completely off and often they rely (heavily) on the 'emotional' factor to even be an enjoyable thing to eat at all. For this reason, we strive to execute them to a high standard without losing any of their nostalgia.

Don't get us wrong, though, these tarts aren't above leveraging on some context to make them seem a touch more incredible than they are. For example, you'll see one savoury-ish tart makes the list here: the Brillat-Savarin and Quince Tart (page 165). As a pastry shop that operates under cafe hours, we believe this tart was never that popular because it was never around at the time of day that you'd want to eat it. We hope that putting it in this section of the book means it gets the glory it deserves in place of (or preferably alongside) a decadent cheese board with a glass of wine in hand.

The correct time and a place for the others will be pretty self-explanatory, but promise we won't hunt you down if you make them whenever you damn-well please.

Hot Cross Bun Tart

The hype around hot cross buns in Melbourne around Easter time is no laughing matter. Every bakery and patisserie makes their version, websites publish full guides on where to snag the best ones and influencers flock all over town to capture their hot cross hauls. So, it begged the question, why couldn't Tarts Anon capitalise on the action?

Hot cross ice-cream, gin and croissants all exist, which goes to show that the flavours of a hot cross bun transcend any format and work together spectacularly. We're not sure if this tart version will ever surpass an actual hot cross bun, but it's definitely something unique to bring to the Easter celebration. Start this recipe a day ahead to soak the raisins.

1 × baked Shortcrust Pastry shell (page 23)

Soaked raisins
70 g (2½ oz) raisins
30 g (1 oz) orange juice
10 g (¼ oz) soft brown sugar
3 g (0.1 oz) brandy
pinch of mixed spice

Hot cross bun cake batter
105 g (3½ oz) natural almond meal
50 g (1¾ oz) plain (all-purpose) flour
45 g (1½ oz) candied orange peel
40 g (1½ oz) candied lemon peel
2 g baking powder
2 g salt

55 g (2 oz) caster (superfine) sugar
75 g (2¾ oz) soft brown sugar
5 g (0.2 oz) mixed spice
120 g (4½ oz) egg
90 g (3 oz) Soaked raisins, see left
120 g (4½ oz) Brown butter (page 111)

Brown butter glaze
180 g (6½ oz) Brown butter (page 111)
400 g (1¹ oz) milk
4 g (0.14 oz) salt
80 g (2¾ oz) soft brown sugar
10 g (¼ oz) pectin X58

Cross
100 g (3½ oz) milk powder

Preheat the oven to 165°C (330°F).

Soaked raisins
Place all ingredients into a small saucepan and bring to a boil, then remove from heat. Decant into a container and let this mixture sit at least overnight to plump up the raisins and infuse them with flavour. Once they are ready to use, drain the liquid and pat dry before adding to the batter.

Hot cross bun cake batter
Weigh the dry ingredients, except the sugars and mixed spice, in a bowl and stir together. Add the eggs, mixed spice and sugar to a separate mixing bowl. Either with a whisk or a stand mixer fitted with a whisk attachment, slowly combine until the sugar has dissolved. You do not want to incorporate any air at this stage, as it tends

to separate when the butter is added and forms a foamy crust, so keep the speed low.

Melt the brown butter in a saucepan. You want this to be warm enough so that the liquid doesn't cool down too quickly, but cool enough so that it doesn't develop any burnt characteristics. If the butter is too hot, it can also fry the egg mixture as you add it, so a thermometer is useful (we aim for roughly 100°C/210°F). Once the butter comes up to temperature, slowly pour it into the egg and sugar mixture (or add little by little, if whisking by hand). Ensure that the mixture is well emulsified, as this will prevent the butter from bleeding out later, giving the cake a greasy texture. Then mix in the dry ingredients and soaked raisins, making sure that there are no lumps suspended throughout the batter. →

To bake

To bake the tart, pour the batter into the pastry shell. Bake the tart for approximately 30 minutes, or until the crust is an even golden brown and the centre of the tart is firm. Remove from the oven and allow to cool inside the tin.

Brown butter glaze

Bring the brown butter, milk and salt to a boil in a small saucepan. Meanwhile, mix the sugar and the pectin together in a bowl to ensure that there are no lumps and the pectin is fully dispersed through the sugar.

Once the liquid is boiling and the butter has melted, add the sugar mix and simmer gently, while whisking, for 20 seconds. Remove from heat and blend this mixture with a hand-held blender. Pour into a container to set.

Cross

Place the milk powder into an oven heated to 150°C (300°F) with the fan turned down low. Leave this to toast for 10 minutes then give a quick stir. Continue to toast for another 5 minutes or until the powder has turned a medium golden colour and has a nutty, buttery smell to it. Allow this to cool and keep in a container.

Take a piece of acetate and cut out a large cross shape to use as your stencil.

To glaze

Once the tart has cooled, it's ready to be glazed (see page 34). Warm 120 g (4½ oz) of the brown butter glaze in a saucepan until just melted. Pour this mixture over 120 g (4½ oz) of cold glaze and mix with a blender until smooth and the texture of thick custard. Pour this over the cake and tilt the tart tin so that the glaze spreads to the edges (for a smooth and clean look, avoid using a spatula). Tap the tart gently on the bench so that it settles in the corners, and place in the fridge for 5–10 minutes to firm up.

Once the glaze is nice and firm, lightly oil either side of the template with spray or wipe on a small amount of oil on it with paper towel (you want to make sure that the powder sticks to the stencil, but the stencil doesn't stick to the glaze!). Place the stencil on top of the set glaze and use a sieve to dust on a light coating of the toasted milk powder. Remove the stencil gently, being sure to not let any of the powder fall on the undusted portions of the glaze, then remove from the tin.

You can choose to apply the stencil to the whole tart, or portion the tart (see page 39) and do this step on each slice. Clearly, this whole step is completely optional, but it is a nice little touch to add to the tart for the easter season!

Mulled Wine Pear and Gingerbread Tart

This tart is inspired by Gareth's favourite ever dessert served at Dinner By Heston Blumenthal, 'The Gingerbread Ice-Cream'. The smoked walnut mousse with a stroopwafel-like orange caramel base was good enough on its own, but paired with vibrant mulled wine pears and a beautifully nuanced gingerbread ice cream, it was such a well-considered dessert that managed to capture Christmas in a mouthful.

Before it was ready for the Tarts Anon menu, we went through quite a few iterations to get the spices in the custard and the acidity of the glaze right, but if you're game enough to try your hand at baking it, you'll agree it's worth the effort. Do take the time to infuse the pears in the mulled wine overnight to get that very deep purple colour to the glaze (and maximum flavour of course!).

1 × baked Shortcrust Pastry shell (page 23)
120 g (4½ oz) Dulce de Leche (page 139)

Poached pear puree
500 g (1 lb 2 oz) packham pears
15 g (½ oz) orange zest
4 g (0.14 oz) cinnamon sticks
2 g star anise
4 g (0.14 oz) cardamom pods
1 g clove
300 g (10½ oz) caster (superfine) sugar
3 g (0.1 oz) vanilla paste, or bean
1 kg (2 lb 3 oz) dry red wine

Mulled wine pear glaze
200 g (7 oz) Poached pear puree, above
200 g (7 oz) reserved poaching wine, see method

50 g (1¾ oz) caster (superfine) sugar
5 g (0.2 oz) pectin NH
5 g (0.2 oz) citric acid

Gingerbread custard
40 g (1½ oz) double (heavy) cream
450 g (1 lb) pouring (whipping) cream
3 g (0.1 oz) orange zest
3 g (0.1 oz) mixed spice
4 g (0.14 oz) ground ginger
125 g (4½ oz) soft brown sugar
180 g (6½ oz) egg yolk
55 g (2 oz) white chocolate callets or buttons

Orange caramel
120 g (4½ oz) Dulce de Leche (page 139)
3 g (0.1 oz) orange zest

Preheat the oven to 125°C (255°F).

Poached pear puree
Peel and core the pears and cut into pieces, approximately 2 × 2 cm (¾ × ¾ in). Tie the aromatics into a bundle of muslin (cheesecloth). Add the red wine, sugar, vanilla paste and aromatics to a pan and bring to a boil over medium heat. Add the pear pieces, turn down to a simmer and cook until the pears can be pierced easily with a paring knife. Turn off the heat. Transfer to a container and allow to sit for 12 hours in the fridge to infuse and to allow the colour to penetrate the fruit before using.

Once the pears are ready, strain the mixture through a fine sieve, reserving the poaching liquid and discarding the bundle of aromatics. Place the cooked pears into a blender and blend until smooth.

Mulled wine pear glaze
Place the measured quantities of pear puree and the reserved poaching wine into a saucepan and bring to a boil. Combine the sugar with the pectin, then whisk it into the liquid and bring to the boil again. Add the citric acid and remove from heat. Blend until smooth, then pass through a fine sieve. Allow the gel to cool and set until firm. →

Gingerbread custard

Place the creams, orange zest, spices and sugar in a saucepan and bring to a simmer, then remove from heat immediately. To temper the egg yolks, add them to a mixing bowl and whisk in a small amount of the hot cream mixture until well incorporated. Add the remaining cream mixture and the white chocolate and use a hand-held blender to blend until the mixture is shiny and smooth – to prevent any air from being incorporated into the mix, keep the head of the blender underneath the surface.

Decant into a jug to use straight away – you want to keep it as warm as possible to ensure the mixture cooks evenly in the oven.

Orange caramel

Mix the dulce de leche and the orange zest together and spread the mixture over the base of the prepared pastry shell, then place in the oven. Pour the custard on top of the caramel layer, ensuring you leave a small gap at the top so that the gel has a little crust to stick to.

To bake

Bake for 30 minutes, or until the custard has a slight wobble in the centre, then remove from the oven and allow to cool.

To glaze

Once the custard has cooled sufficiently, melt the mulled wine pear gel in a small saucepan over a low heat (you can pop the tart into the fridge to the fridge to help the custard to firm up, which will also help the gel to set faster). Once the gel has fully melted and has started to simmer slightly, weigh out 220 g (8 oz) of the gel into a measuring jug. Pour the glaze over the tart in a circular motion (see page 37), starting from the inside and moving outwards. Gently transfer the tart into the fridge and allow to set.

Once the gel is firm to the touch, remove the tart the tin and portion into slices with a hot, sharp knife (see page 39).

Chocolate and Chestnut Tart

Flavour wise, chestnuts are a difficult ingredient to get the most out of because when used in large quantities their texture can become unpleasant. It therefore becomes a fine balancing act to get the right amount of chestnut flavour into a tart without it becoming too thick and pasty in the mouth. Chocolate, chestnuts and redcurrants are all very Christmassy, and we even dust this one with gold powder at the shop because we're big fat liars who do, sometimes, believe in nice garnishes, especially at Christmas. Omit the gold leaf, if you like, and simply tell people you 'don't believe in garnishes' – they will believe you.

1 × baked Shortcrust Pastry shell (page 23)
roasted chestnuts, for grating
gold powder (completely optional, obviously)

Redcurrant jam
300 g (10½ oz) redcurrant juice
210 g (7½ oz) caster (superfine) sugar
5 g (0.2 oz) pectin jaune
2 g citric acid
15 g (½ oz) water

Chestnut puree
150 g (5½ oz) whole chestnuts, fresh or frozen
125 g (4½ oz) milk
140 g (5 oz) pouring (whipping) cream
20 g (¾ oz) caster (superfine) sugar
5 g (0.2 oz) salt

Chestnut glaze
125 g (4½ oz) Chestnut puree, left
125 g (4½ oz) milk
90 g (3 oz) pouring (whipping) cream
3.5 g (0.12 oz) pectin C58
25 g (1 oz) caster (superfine) sugar

Chocolate cake batter
140 g (5 oz) natural almond meal
20 g (¾ oz) cocoa powder
90 g (3 oz) plain (all purpose) flour
3 g (0.1 oz) baking powder
2 g salt
185 g (6½ oz) caster (superfine) sugar
160 g (5½ oz) egg
155 g (5½ oz) Brown butter (page 111)

Preheat the oven to 165°C (330°F).

Redcurrant jam
To make the redcurrant jam, bring the redcurrant juice to a boil in a medium saucepan. Whisk together the caster sugar and the pectin and mix into the boiling liquid, then turn down to a medium heat. Mix the citric acid with the water and set aside. Continue to cook the jam until it reaches 106°C (223°F), then add the citric acid solution and bring to the boil once more. Decant this mixture into a bowl or container and reserve for later.

Chestnut puree
Add the chestnuts (plus a couple extra to grate over the top of the finished tart) to a baking tray (sheet) and roast for 30 minutes, or until a medium brown colour. Then place

in a saucepan with the milk, cream, sugar and salt and bring to a boil. Using a hand-held blender, blitz the chestnuts to a smooth puree and keep warm.

Chestnut glaze
Place 125 g (4½ oz) of the chestnut puree into a saucepan with the milk and cream. Bring to a boil over medium heat. Mix the pectin and sugar in a small bowl and add to the chestnut mixture. Return the mixture to a boil, then remove from the heat and blend with a hand-held blender until smooth. Decant this into a container and cover the surface of the liquid with plastic wrap to prevent a skin from forming. Cool in the fridge. →

Chocolate cake batter

Weigh the dry ingredients, except the sugar, in a separate bowl and stir them together. Add the eggs and sugar to a separate mixing bowl. Either with a whisk or a stand mixer fitted with a whisk attachment, slowly combine until the sugar has dissolved. You do not want to incorporate any air at this stage, as it tends to separate when the butter is added and forms a foamy crust, so keep the speed low.

Melt the brown butter in a saucepan. You want this to be warm enough so that the liquid doesn't cool down too quickly, but cool enough so that it doesn't develop any burnt characteristics. If the butter is too hot, it can also fry the egg mixture as you add it, so a thermometer is useful (we aim for roughly 100°C/210°F).

Once the butter comes up to temperature, slowly pour it into the egg and sugar mixture (or add little by little, if whisking by hand). Ensure that the mixture is well emulsified, as this will prevent the butter from bleeding out later, giving the cake a greasy texture. Finally, mix in the dry ingredients, making sure that there are no lumps suspended throughout the batter.

To bake

Spread 100 g (3½ oz) of the redcurrant jam over the base of the pastry shell, then pour 500 g (1 lb 2 oz) of chocolate cake batter on top. Place the tart into the oven to bake for approximately 30 minutes, or until the crust is an even colour and the centre of the tart is firm. Remove from the oven and allow to cool inside the tin.

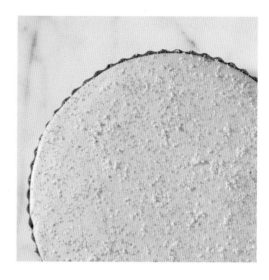

To glaze

Once the tart has cooled, it's ready to be glazed (see page 34). Warm 150 g (5½ oz) of the chestnut glaze in a saucepan until just melted. Pour this mixture over 150 g (5½ oz) of cold glaze and mix with a hand-held blender until smooth and the texture of thick custard. Pour this over the baked cake layer and tilt the tart so that the glaze spreads to the edges (for a smooth and clean look, avoid using a spatula). Tap the tart gently on the bench so that it settles in the knuckles of the pastry shell, and place in the fridge for 5–10 minutes to firm up.

Once the glaze is nice and firm, remove the tart from the tin and portion the tart into slices with a hot, sharp knife (see page 39). Finish by grating fine layer of roasted chestnut on top and dust lightly with gold powder, if using, for that festive flair.

Passionfruit, Rhubarb and Strawberry Pavlova Tart

The idea here was to make a meringue reminiscent of a pavlova and sit it atop a custard tart. Achieving this is quite a feat because the meringue has to be baked separately so it can dry on the outside and go crispy like a pavlova. This is different to a meringue that you might put on top of a lemon pie, which is either torched or baked and which allows the egg whites to set but not turn crisp. The sense of accomplishment when we finally got the process for this down pat was probably one of our most satisfying achievements to date. But don't let this put you off – by carefully following the recipe it should all come together for you on the first try. If not, at least you'll have some kind of meringue pie.

The strawberry and passionfruit powders are available from any good providore. The nougasec used in the meringue is an additive made of a mixture of starches, lactose and glucose that helps stop the absorption of sugar. You can purchase it online.

1 × baked Shortcrust Pastry shell (page 23)
strawberry powder, for dusting
passionfruit powder, for dusting

Strawberry jam
200 g (7 oz) strawberries
70 g (2½ oz) caster (superfine) sugar, plus 70 g (2½ oz)
4 g (0.14 oz) pectin jaune
8 g (0.3 oz) citric acid
3 g (0.1 oz) water

Rhubarb jam
200 g (7 oz) rhubarb
80 g (2¾ oz) caster (superfine) sugar, plus 80 g (2¾ oz)
3 g (0.1 oz) pectin jaune

3 g (0.1 oz) citric acid
8 g (0.3 oz) water

Meringue
90 g (3 oz) egg white
7 g (¼ oz) nougasec
10 g (¼ oz) cornflour (cornstarch)
180 g (6½ oz) caster sugar

Passionfruit custard
90 g (3 oz) passionfruit juice
80 g (2¾ oz) pouring (whipping) cream
95 g (3¼ oz) double (heavy) cream
130 g (4½ oz) caster (superfine) sugar
50 g (1¾ oz) egg
100 g (3½ oz) egg yolk

Strawberry jam
Put the strawberries into a small saucepan along with 70 g (2½ oz) of the sugar and bring to a gentle simmer. Mix the remaining sugar with the pectin and whisk into the strawberry mixture. Continue to cook until the strawberries collapse and the liquid is almost gone, then remove from heat. Using a hand-held blender, blend until there are no more lumps of fruit. Mix the citric acid with the water and allow to dissolve, then set aside. Return the strawberry mixture to the heat and continue to cook until the mixture becomes thick, whisking often to avoid it catching on a the bottom of the saucepan.

This would drastically change the flavour and colour of the jam. When the mixture reaches 107°C (225°F) on a thermometer, whisk in the citric acid mixture, then remove from heat and pour into a container to set.

Rhubarb jam
Cut the rhubarb into 2 cm (¾ in) pieces and place into a small saucepan along with 80 g (2¾ oz) of the sugar and bring to a gentle simmer. Once soft, remove the rhubarb from the pan with a slotted spoon and drain well. Mix the remaining sugar with the pectin and whisk into the syrup. →

Continue to cook until the syrup reaches 107°C (225°F) on a thermometer. Meanwhile mix the citric acid with the water in a small bowl and allow to dissolve. Once the syrup comes up to temperature, stir in the rhubarb and the citric acid. Remove from the heat and pour into a container to set. When the jams are still quite warm, weigh out 150 g (5½ oz) of the rhubarb and 150 g (5½ oz) of the strawberry jam. Mix the two jams together before allowing to set in the fridge (you will have enough jam left over to make a second tart, if desired).

Meringue

Place the egg whites and the nougasec into the bowl of a stand mixer fixed with the whisk attachment and begin mixing on a medium speed. Mix the cornflour and sugar together in a bowl. When the egg whites start to foam slightly on the surface, slowly rain the sugar mixture in while mixing. Turn the mixer up to high once the sugar has been added and continue to whisk until the meringue is glossy and stiff.

Next, bake the meringue in a tart tin so it's ready to place onto the custard layer later. To line the tart tin, cut a strip of baking paper (or two shorter ones stuck together) to 80 × 5 cm (31½ × 2 in). Cut another piece of paper into a circle 25 cm (10 in) in diameter, and place into the bottom of your tart tin. Spray either side very lightly with oil spray, and do the same with the strips, wrapping them around the inside of the tin. These will not stick directly to the edge of the tin but try to keep to the shape of the tin as much as possible.

Once the meringue is ready, place it into a large piping bag with a 2 cm (¾ in) round nozzle (this larger nozzle is preferable – but you can also cut the top of a disposable piping bag to this size). Pipe the meringue directly into the edges of the tart tin in a smooth consistent line – this will ensure that the edges of the meringue are nice and straight and will eliminate any gaps between the custard and the shell. Fill the rest of the shell with the meringue in an even layer, then use a palette knife to spread the meringue around to create some natural 'flowy' peaks. This is entirely optional, but the more texture the surface has, the more crispiness you will get.

1st bake

Bake the meringue in an oven set to 100°C (210°F) for 25 minutes or until firm and dry (it will dry out and become even firmer as they cool, so bear this in mind). Remove the meringue from the tart tin once cooled (the meringue will keep for up to a week in an airtight container). Increase the oven temperature to 125°C (255°F) to preheat for baking the tart.

Passionfruit custard

Add the passionfruit juice, creams, and sugar to a saucepan and bring to a simmer, then remove immediately. To temper the whole eggs and egg yolks, add them to a mixing bowl and whisk in a small amount of the hot cream mixture until well incorporated, then add the remaining cream mix. Using a hand-held blender, blend until the mixture is shiny and smooth – to ensure no air is incorporated, keep the head of the blender submerged. Strain the custard into a measuring jug and let sit for 5 minutes for all the impurities to rise to the top, then remove them with a ladle or slotted spoon.

Once the surface is clear of bubbles, pour the custard into the tart shell straight away – you want to keep it as warm as possible to ensure the mixture cooks evenly in the oven.

2nd bake

Bake the tart for 30 minutes, or until the custard is slightly wobbly in the centre, then remove from the oven and allow to cool. Once the custard has completely cooled, remove the tart from the tin. Place the meringue on top of the cooled custard and portion the tart into slices with a hot, sharp knife (see page 39). Dust the top of the meringue with a small amount of the passionfruit and strawberry powders before serving.

Eggnog and Fruit Mince Tart

We made this for Tarts Anon's first Christmas and the recipe has been more or less the same ever since. When it landed on the menu, Catherine appealed for people to taste-test it to make sure they wouldn't be disappointed on the big day. One of our delightful taste-testers had this to say about the tart and we think it sums it up very nicely: 'This melt-in-your-mouth indulgence has me lighting candles while I hang the Christmas tree lights. It's boozy, it's boujie, it's pure brilliance and it's a 10 from me.' – @Burritobek

The fruit mince recipe is best made ahead of time, ideally one month before its intended use. This allows the fruit to mature and ferment slightly, and for the spices to infuse and the flavour to develop. It will also oxidise slightly and the mix will take on the deep colour and flavour that is synonymous with fruit mince. This step is obviously optional, as there are many great companies that produce lovely fruit mince that is available for purchase.

---

1 × baked Shortcrust Pastry shell (page 23)
nutmeg, for grating

Fruit mince
200 g (7 oz) butter
350 g (12½ oz) pink lady apples, peeled,
    cored and cut in 2 cm (¾ in) dice
350 g (12½ oz) raisins
350 g (12½ oz) soft brown sugar
150 g (5½ oz) candied orange zest
200 g (7 oz) orange juice
100 g (3½ oz) lemon juice
30 g (1 oz) lemon zest

150 g (5½ oz) brandy
20 g (¾ oz) mixed spice
10 g (¼ oz) cornflour (cornstarch)
20 g (¾ oz) water

Eggnog custard
570 g (1 lb 4 oz) pouring (whipping) cream
50 g (1¾ oz) double (heavy) cream
4 g (0.14 oz) mixed spice
2 g vanilla paste
70 g (2½ oz) brandy
160 g (5½ oz) soft brown sugar
260 g (9 oz) egg yolk

Preheat the oven to 165°C (330°F).

Fruit mince
Melt the butter in a saucepan, then add all the ingredients except for the cornflour and water. Bring the mixture to a boil then turn down to a simmer and continue to cook on a low heat, stirring occasionally, until the liquid is all but evaporated. Mix the water with the cornflour and stir to form a loose slurry, then add to the boiling fruit mince. Return the mixture to the boil and then begin to whisk for 30 seconds – then remove from heat and pour into a container to cool.

Eggnog custard
Place the creams, spices, vanilla, brandy and sugar in a saucepan and bring to a simmer, then remove immediately. To temper the egg yolks, add them to a mixing bowl and whisk in a small amount of the hot cream mixture

until well incorporated. Add the remaining cream mixture and use a hand-held blender to blend until the mixture is shiny and smooth – to prevent any air from being incorporated into the mix, keep the head of the blender underneath the surface. Decant into a measuring jug to use straight away – you want to keep it as warm as possible to ensure the mixture cooks evenly in the oven.

To bake
Spread the fruit mince over the base of the pastry shell. Place the prepared tart into the oven, then pour the custard over the fruit mince layer. Bake for 30 minutes, or until the custard is slightly wobbly in the centre, then remove from the oven and allow to cool. Once the custard has completely cooled, remove the tart from the tin and portion into slices (see page 39). Finish each slice by grating a fine layer of nutmeg on top.

Pineapple Tart

We made this tart for a Lunar New Year special as a nod to the traditional pineapple tarts that are eaten during this time. Many of our chefs perfected the pineapple carving technique used in this recipe during their time at Dinner by Heston Blumenthal, as roasted pineapple was a key component of one of the restaurant's most famous desserts, the 'Tipsy Cake'. It's the most efficient way to get rid of the undesirable parts of the pineapple and the most economic because you're removing the least amount of the usable flesh. It may take a bit of investigating and some trial and error, but with a bit of practice, this can be a very therapeutic task! Once you learn how to carve pineapples this way, it's a skill you will take to the grave.

1 × baked Shortcrust Pastry shell (page 23)
1 medium-sized pineapple
    (preferably the golden variety)

Caramel glaze
170 g (6 oz) caster (superfine) sugar,
    plus 10 g (¼ oz)
210 g (7½ oz) apple juice
3 g (0.1 oz) pectin NH
1 g salt
2 g citric acid

Almond cake batter
140 g (5 oz) natural almond meal
75 g (2¾ oz) plain (all-purpose) flour
3 g (0.1 oz) baking powder
2 g salt
185 g (6½ oz) sugar
160 g (5½ oz) egg
160 g (5½ oz) Brown butter (page 111)

Preheat the oven to 165°C (330°F).

Caramel glaze
Make a direct caramel by heating a medium-sized pot over low heat and gradually adding 170 g (6 oz) of the sugar one layer at a time, allowing each layer to fully melt and start to caramelise before adding the next. Once the sugar has fully dissolved and the caramel is a medium-brown colour, add the apple juice a little at a time and bring to a boil. Mix the remaining sugar with the pectin and salt, then add this to the boiling mixture. Once this returns to the boil, add the citric acid, then whisk until fully dissolved. Pass this mixture through a fine sieve and allow to set in a container in the fridge.

To prepare the pineapple
First trim off the top and bottom of the fruit, then remove as little of the tough outer skin as possible, while ensuring there is no green left on the flesh. Then, using a sharp serrated paring knife, follow the direction of the eyelets and make a shallow incision approximately 1 cm (½ in) deep on the underside of each. Each eye is only a few millimetres deep in the fruit, so to avoid your wedges falling apart, try and keep your incisions nice and shallow. Once each row of eyelets has a cut on the underside, turn the pineapple upside down and make another 1 cm (½ in) cut on the other side of the eyelet at an angle to remove the flesh around each one.

Once all the eyes have been removed, cut the pineapple in half lengthways. Place each half cut-side down and cut in half again lengthways. Cut each quarter in half, and then rotate 90 degrees and cut into shorter wedges, each should be approximately 10 cm (4 in) long and 4–5 cm (1½–2 in) thick at its widest point. Place these chunks on their side, trim off the fibrous core and trim the chunks down to a triangular wedge shape – ensuring that your 'troughs' are not so deep that these pieces fall apart. Put these to the side. →

Almond cake batter

Weigh the dry ingredients, except the sugar, in a separate bowl and stir them together. Add the egg and sugar to a separate mixing bowl. Either with a whisk or a stand mixer fitted with a whisk attachment, slowly combine until the sugar has dissolved. You do not want to incorporate any air at this stage, as it tends to separate when the butter is added and forms a foamy crust, so keep the speed low.

Melt the brown butter in a saucepan. You want this to be warm enough so that the liquid doesn't cool down too quickly, but cool enough so that it doesn't develop any burnt characteristics. If the butter is too hot, it can also fry the egg mixture as you add it, so a thermometer is useful (we aim for roughly 100°C/210°F).

Once the butter comes up to temperature, slowly pour it into the egg and sugar mixture (or add little by little, if whisking by hand). Ensure that the mixture is well emulsified, as this will prevent the butter from bleeding out later, giving the cake a greasy texture. Finally, mix in the dry ingredients, making sure that there are no lumps suspended throughout the batter.

To assemble and bake

To assemble the tart, pour the batter into the pastry shell. Its best to allow this to cool slightly so that the mix stiffens up and your pineapples stay nice and tall. Then, place ten pineapple pieces (or however many slices you would like your tart to have) evenly around the batter so that it sits at the centre of each slice.

Bake the tart for approximately 30 minutes, or until the crust is an even golden brown and the centre of the tart is firm. Remove from the oven and allow to cool inside the tin.

To glaze

Bring the caramel glaze to a boil in a small saucepan. Using a large pastry brush, brush a thick layer over the top of the tart and allow to set for a few minutes.

Once the glaze is nice and firm, remove the tart from the tin and cut into portions with a hot, sharp knife (see page 39).

White Chocolate, Raspberry and Pistachio Tart

If you want to make a tart that sells well on Valentine's Day, then make it pink, load it with some kind of expensive ingredient and portion it into quarters for couples to share. That's what we did, anyway, and it turned out pretty well. In all fairness, though, we didn't really need an excuse to make this tart; white chocolate, pistachio and raspberries are a classic combination of flavours that work exceptionally well in tart form and in hindsight, there was really no need to make a gimmick out of it.

1 × baked Shortcrust Pastry shell (page 23)

Pistachio puree
80 g (2¾ oz) pistachios, shelled

Raspberry jam
390 g (14 oz) raspberries
105 g (3½ oz) caster (superfine) sugar,
    plus 105 g (3½ oz)
6 g (0.2 oz) pectin jaune
5 g (0.2 oz) citric acid
12 g (0.4 oz) water

White chocolate and raspberry glaze
150 g (5½ oz) pouring (whipping) cream
200 g (7 oz) milk

90 g (3 oz) raspberry puree, above
2 g salt
5 g (0.2 oz) pectin X58
50 g (1¾ oz) caster (superfine) sugar
100 g (3½ oz) white chocolate callets
    or buttons

Pistachio cake batter
85 g (3 oz) natural almond meal
55 g (2 oz) plain (all-purpose) flour
4 g (0.14 oz) salt
2 g baking powder
140 g (5 oz) golden caster sugar
140 g (5 oz) egg
80 g (2¾ oz) Pistachio puree, left
80 g (2¾ oz) Brown butter (page 111)

Preheat the oven to 120°C (250°F)

Pistachio puree
Place the pistachios on an oven tray (sheet) and toast in the oven for 45 minutes. This will allow the moisture to escape from the pistachios without changing their vibrant colour. While the pistachios are still hot, blend in a food processor until smooth.

Increase the oven to 165°C (330°F) to preheat for baking the tart.

Raspberry jam
Put the raspberries in a narrow measuring jug or container and blend with a hand-held blender until very smooth. Set aside 90 g (3 oz) of the puree to use for the glaze. Add the remaining raspberry puree and 105 g (3½ oz) of the sugar to a medium-sized saucepan and bring to the boil. Whisk the

remaining sugar and the pectin together, and rain into the puree once boiled. Mix the citric acid and water together in a bowl and set aside. Continue to cook the raspberry mixture until it reaches 107°C (225°F) on a thermometer, then stir in the citric acid solution. Pour this mixture into a container to set.

White chocolate and raspberry glaze
Weigh the cream, milk, reserved raspberry puree and salt in a large saucepan. Then, weigh the pectin and the sugar in a separate container and set aside. Bring the cream mixture to a boil, then add the pectin mixture and whisk for 20 seconds. Add the white chocolate, then remove from heat. Blend the mixture with a hand-held blender until smooth and glossy. Decant into a container and allow to set before using. →

Pistachio cake batter

Weigh the dry ingredients, except the sugar, in a separate bowl and stir them together. Add the eggs and sugar to a separate mixing bowl. Either with a whisk or a stand mixer fitted with a whisk attachment, slowly combine until the sugar has dissolved. You do not want to incorporate any air at this stage, as it tends to separate when the butter is added and forms a foamy crust, so keep the speed low.

Melt the brown butter in a saucepan. You want this to be warm enough so that the liquid doesn't cool down too quickly, but cool enough so that it doesn't develop any burnt characteristics. If the butter is too hot, it can also fry the egg mixture as you add it, so a thermometer is useful (we aim for roughly 100°C/210°F).

Once the butter comes up to temperature, stir in the pistachio puree until combined. Slowly pour this into the egg and sugar mixture (or add little by little, if whisking by hand). Ensure that the mixture is well emulsified, as this will prevent the butter from bleeding out later, giving the cake a greasy texture. Finally, mix in the dry ingredients, making sure that there are no lumps suspended throughout the batter.

To bake

Spread 100 g (3½ oz) of the raspberry jam over the base of the tart, then pour the batter on top. Bake the tart for approximately 30 minutes, or until the crust is an even colour and the centre of the tart is firm. Remove from the oven and allow to cool inside the tin.

To glaze

Once the tart has cooled, it's ready to be glazed (see page 34). Warm 120 g (4½ oz) of the white chocolate glaze in a saucepan until just melted. Pour this mixture over 120 g (4½ oz) of cold glaze and mix with a hand-held blender until smooth and the texture of thick custard. Pour this over the baked cake and tilt the tart so that the glaze spreads to the edges (for a smooth and clean look, avoid using a spatula). Tap the tart gently on the bench so that it settles in the knuckles of the crust, and place in the fridge for 5–10 minutes to firm up.

Once the glaze is nice and firm, portion the tart into slices with a hot, sharp knife (see page 39).

Chocolate, Orange and Whiskied Pecan Tart

This is a special occasion tart but we're going to let you choose the festivity. We first made it as a Father's Day special, then because it was so popular, brought it back for the public holiday following the Queen's passing and then the AFL Grand Final. We can all agree that this multi-purpose tart screams 'You're a good dad', 'National day of mourning', 'We love sport', and much, much more. Actually, it was also on the 2022 Christmas menu. I'm sure you can find a suitable occasion for it too (we'd be worried if you couldn't). Furthermore, it makes a great 'occasion' tart, because it's a touch more complex in its construction and, as all good celebrations do, also contains a bit of booze. You can omit the whisky by replacing it with orange juice in the soaking syrup for a booze-free alternative.

1 × baked Shortcrust Pastry shell (page 23)

Orange caramel
200 g (7 oz) Dulce de Leche (page 139)
8 g (0.3 oz) orange zest
2 g salt

Pecan puree
150 g (5½ oz) pecans

Pecan praline
100 g (3½ oz) pecans
70 g (2½ oz) caster sugar

Whisky syrup
60 g (2 oz) whisky
60 g (2 oz) caster sugar
60 g (2 oz) water

Pecan cake batter
85 g (3 oz) natural almond meal
35 g (1¼ oz) plain (all-purpose) flour
2 g baking powder
3 g (0.1 oz) salt
55 g (2 oz) Pecan puree, left
60 g (2 oz) golden caster (superfine) sugar
50 g (1¾ oz) soft brown sugar
95 g (3¼ oz) egg
65 g (2¼ oz) Brown butter (page 111)

Pecan 'gianduja'
130 g (4½ oz) milk chocolate callets or buttons
45 g (1½ oz) Pecan puree, left
5 g (0.2 oz) salt
5 g (0.2 oz) orange zest
55 g (2 oz) Pecan praline, left
55 g (2 oz) feuilletine (see page 97)

Preheat the oven to 165°C (330°F)

Orange caramel
To make the caramel, mix the dulce de leche in a bowl with the orange zest and salt. Spread this mixture over the base of the pastry shell.

Pecan puree
Add the pecans to a baking tray (sheet) and toast until a deep golden brown. While still warm, blend the nuts in a food processor until smooth and runny. Set this mixture aside – you'll need to use it for the cake batter and the 'gianduja' layer.

Pecan praline
Start by chopping the pecans into small pieces, approximately 1 cm (½ in) in size. Place on a baking tray (sheet) and toast as for the puree. Make a direct caramel by heating a saucepan on the stove and gradually adding the sugar one layer at a time, allowing each layer to fully melt and start to caramelise before adding the next. Once the sugar has fully dissolved and the caramel is a medium-brown colour, add the still-warm pecans and stir through the caramel then pour out onto a tray lined with baking paper. →

When this cools, use a rolling pin to first break up the praline, then smash into smaller pieces. For this, you can use either a knife to chop it into pieces roughly 5 mm (¼ in) in size, or pulse quickly in a food processor. Set the praline aside in an airtight container as it tends to become sticky very quickly. Increase the oven heat to 165°C (330°F) to preheat for baking the tart.

Whisky syrup
In a saucepan, bring all of the ingredients to a boil to dissolve the sugar. Ensure the mixture is warm when you pour it onto the cake later, as it will help to absorb into the cake that bit easier.

Pecan cake batter
Weigh the dry ingredients, except the sugars, in a bowl and stir them together. Add the eggs and sugars to a separate mixing bowl. Either with a whisk or a stand mixer fitted with a whisk attachment, slowly combine until the sugar has dissolved. You do not want to incorporate any air at this stage, as it tends to separate when the butter is added and forms a foamy crust, so keep the speed low.

Melt the brown butter in a saucepan. You want this to be warm enough so that the liquid doesn't cool down too quickly, but cool enough so that it doesn't develop any burnt characteristics. If the butter is too hot, it can also fry the egg mixture as you add it, so a thermometer is useful (we aim for roughly 100°C/210°F).

Once the butter comes up to temperature, stir in the pecan puree, then slowly pour this into the egg and sugar mixture (or add little by little, if whisking by hand). Ensure that the mixture is well emulsified, as this will prevent the butter from bleeding out later, giving the cake a greasy texture. Finally, mix in the dry ingredients, making sure that there are no lumps suspended throughout the batter.

To bake
Pour the cake batter over the caramel layer inside the tart and bake for 30 minutes, or until nice and firm. It may seem a little overcooked, but it's important that it's slightly on the drier side. Use a fork to poke some holes all over the top of the cake while still hot so that some of the steam is released. Next, reheat the whisky syrup and brush on top of the cake until it has all absorbed.

Pecan 'gianduja'
Place the chocolate, pecan puree, salt and orange zest in a heat proof bowl set on top of a pot of boiling water and stir until melted. Add the praline chunks and the feuilletine flakes and stir until combined. Pour this on top of the cooled tart, spreading it right to the edges. Give the tart a tap on the bench so that the chocolate layer evens out, then put it in the fridge for 15 minutes to set.

Once the gianduja is cool and firm, remove the tart from the tin and portion into slices (see page 39).

Brillat-Savarin and Quince Tart

When we first put this tart on the menu, we had to explain to some of our customers what Brillat-Savarin is and why in god's name would we put it in a custard – let alone in a tart. We landed on this description: 'Imagine grabbing all the good bits on a cheese plate – the cracker or maybe an oatcake, the quince jam, some nuts, and of course the cheese – then eating them all at once.' This is a tart for the people who order a cheese board instead of dessert. It is by no means the most popular tart on the menu when it comes around, but everyone who tried it loved it and begged us for it to come back. There is, however, one simple rule: If you make it home, you must enjoy it with a glass of wine.

1 × baked Shortcrust Pastry shell (page 23)
50 g (1¾ oz) blanched hazelnuts

Quince jam
150 g (5½ oz) caster (superfine) sugar, plus 50 g (1¾ oz)
450 g (1 lb) water
3 g (0.1 oz) pectin jaune
3 large ripe quinces
5 g (0.2 oz) citric acid

Honey cake batter
70 g (2½ oz) almond meal

20 g (¾ oz) flour
1 g baking powder
1 g salt
40 g (1½ oz) caster (superfine) sugar
75 g (2¾ oz) egg
60 g (2 oz) honey
85 g (3 oz) Brown butter (page 111)

Brillat-Savarin custard
90 g (3 oz) Brillat-Savarin cheese
85 g (3 oz) egg yolk
250 g (9 oz) pouring (whipping) cream
3 g (0.1 oz) salt

Preheat the oven to 165°C (330°F).

Quince jam
Bring 150 g (5½ oz) of the sugar and the water to a boil in a medium saucepan. Mix the remaining sugar with the pectin in a small bowl and set aside. Peel and quarter the quinces, then remove the core and reserve, along with the peel. Cut the quince quarters into 2 cm (¾ in) pieces, place into the syrup and simmer until they are soft and start to turn pink. Strain the quince, reserving the syrup, and place onto a baking tray (sheet) lined with baking paper.

Bake the quinces for approximately 15 minutes. Once the baked quince is firm and has lost all surface moisture, remove from the oven and place into a tall measuring jug. Use a hand-held blender to blend the fruit until smooth.

While the quince is baking, return the syrup to the saucepan, add the reserved peel and cores and bring to the boil. Continue to cook until the syrup has turned a deep red colour, strain and discard the peel and cores and bring the syrup to boil again. Whisk the sugar and pectin mixture into the boiling syrup and continue to cook until it has reached 106°C (225°F). Stir in the quince puree and the citric acid, bring to the boil one last time, then remove from heat and pour into a container to set.

Honey cake batter
Weigh the dry ingredients, except the sugar, in a separate bowl and stir them together. Add the eggs, honey and sugar to a separate mixing bowl. Either with a whisk or a stand mixer fitted with a whisk attachment, slowly combine until the honey and sugar have dissolved. →

TARTS ANON

You do not want to incorporate any air at this stage, as it tends to separate when the butter is added and forms a foamy crust, so keep the speed low.

Melt the brown butter in a saucepan. You want this to be warm enough so that the liquid doesn't cool down too quickly, but cool enough so that it doesn't develop any burnt characteristics. If the butter is too hot, it can also fry the egg mixture as you add it, so a thermometer is useful (we aim for roughly 100°C/210°F).

Once the butter comes up to temperature, slowly pour it into the egg mixture (or add little by little, if whisking by hand). Ensure that the mixture is well emulsified, as this will prevent the butter from bleeding out later, giving the cake a greasy texture. Finally, mix in the dry ingredients, making sure that there are no lumps suspended throughout the batter.

To bake
Pour the batter into the pastry shell. Bake the tart for approximately 18 minutes, or until the crust is an even golden brown and the centre of the tart is firm. Remove from the oven and allow to cool inside the tin.

Once the cake layer has cooled, spread 150 g (5½ oz) of quince jam over the top. Meanwhile, add the hazelnuts to a baking tray (sheet) and roast in the oven for 12 minutes.

After toasting the hazelnuts, reduce the oven heat to 120°C (250°F).

Brillat-Savarin custard
Place the tart into the preheated oven for approximately 5 minutes ahead of baking the custard. This allows the bottom half of the tart to be warm so that the custard will begin cooking straight away.

To make the Brillat-Savarin custard, place the cheese and the egg yolks together in a tall measuring jug and set aside. Bring the cream to the boil with the salt, then pour this hot mixture over the egg and cheese. Using a hand-held blender, blitz the custard until it is smooth and glossy.

To bake
Pour the custard over the jam layer and bake in the oven for 15 minutes, or until set. Allow to cool at room temperature, then remove the tart from the tin. Portion the tart into slices with a hot, sharp knife (see page 39) and finish by using a microplane to dust an even layer of grated roasted hazelnuts on top.

Pumpkin and Spiced Caramel Tart

Let us assure you this is unlike any pumpkin pie you've had before, and that's intentional. Originally, we created this tart for Halloween, but it's become a popular Thanksgiving option for any American and Canadian expats living in Australia. We find that people aren't that adventurous when it comes to tart flavours in the shop (the more 'out there' combos don't sell as well as the classics) but the exception is this tart, genuinely due to word of mouth. Also, we bully people into buying it because it's that good. It's one of the easiest tarts to make and one of the most special.

1 × baked Shortcrust Pastry shell (page 23)

Pumpkin puree
500 g (1 lb 2 oz) grey pumpkin
  (kabocha squash), or similar

Spiced caramel
2 g salt
2 g cinnamon
2 g nutmeg
1 g clove

1 g ground ginger
270 g (9½ oz) Dulce de Leche (page 139)

Pumpkin custard
280 g (10 oz) Pumpkin puree, left
65 g (2¼ oz) Brown butter (page 111)
240 g (8½ oz) pouring cream
115 g (4 oz) golden caster (superfine) sugar
8 g (0.3 oz) salt
200 g (7 oz) egg yolk

Preheat the oven to 180°C (360°F)

Pumpkin puree
Cut the pumpkin into large wedges and remove the seeds. Place on a baking tray (sheet) lined with baking paper, then bake for 45 minutes, or until soft. Once the pumpkin is soft, remove from the oven and allow to cool. Then remove the skin and place in a blender and blitz until smooth for approximately 3 minutes. Set this mix aside.

Reduce the oven heat to 125°C (255°F) to preheat for baking the tart.

Spiced caramel
Next, mix the spices and salt into the dulce de leche with a maryse spatula, and spread over the base of the pastry shell.

Pumpkin custard
Add the pumpkin puree, brown butter, cream, sugar and salt to a large saucepan and bring to a simmer, then remove from

heat immediately. To temper the egg yolks, add them to a mixing bowl and whisk in a small amount of the hot pumpkin mixture until well incorporated. Add the remaining pumpkin mixture and blend with a hand-held blender until shiny and smooth – to prevent any air from being incorporated into the mix, keep the head of the blender underneath the surface. Decant into a jug to use straight away – you want to keep it as warm as possible to ensure the mixture cooks evenly in the oven.

To bake
Place the prepared tart shell into the oven and pour the custard over the caramel layer. Bake for 30 minutes or until the custard is slightly wobbly in the centre, then remove from the oven and allow to cool.

Once the custard has completely cooled, remove the tart from the tin and portion the into slices with a hot, sharp knife (see page 39).

St Honoré Tart

Filming *Dessert Masters* in 2023 was an incredible experience, not only for the friendships Gareth made with his competitors, who are some of the best pastry chefs in Australia, but also for the inspiration it gave us to continue pushing the boundaries at Tarts Anon.

This tart was inspired by the classic French pastry, Gâteau Saint-Honoré, named after the patron saint of pâtissiers. Our version includes a hazelnut caramel base, baked vanilla custard, vanilla crème diplomate and is adorned with caramelised profiteroles filled with vanilla crème pâtissière. This one is the ultimate 'any celebration' celebration tart.

We use a St Honorè piping (pastry) tip here – see page 91 for our hack if you don't have one.

1 × baked Shortcrust Pastry shell (page 23)

Hazelnut caramel
80 g (2¾ oz) hazelnuts
80 g (2¾ oz) caster (superfine) sugar
100 g (3½ oz) Dulce de Leche (page 111)

Profiteroles
75 g (2¾ oz) butter
8 g (0.3 oz) caster sugar
80 g (2¾ oz) milk
75 g (2¾ oz) water
3 g (0.1 oz) salt
90 g (3 oz) flour
165 g (6 oz) egg

Vanilla crème pâtissière
455 g (1 lb) milk
115 g (4 oz) caster sugar
2 g vanilla paste
70 g (2½ oz) egg yolk

30 g (1 oz) cornflour (cornstarch)
30 g (1 oz) butter

Caramel
150 g (5½ oz) caster (superfine) sugar

Vanilla custard
475 g (1 lb 1 oz) pouring (whipping) cream
55 g (2 oz) double (heavy) cream
40 g (1½ oz) cream cheese
140 g (5 oz) soft brown sugar
6 g (0.2 oz) vanilla paste or
    1 vanilla bean, scraped
1 g coffee beans
195 g (7 oz) egg yolk

Crème diplomate
125 g (4½ oz) double (heavy) cream
175 g (6 oz) pouring (whipping) cream
350 g (12½ oz) Vanilla crème pâtissière, above

Preheat the oven to 165°C (330°F).

Hazelnut caramel
Roast the hazelnuts on a baking tray (sheet) for approximately 15 minutes. Once they are a medium golden brown, remove them from the oven and set aside. If your hazelnuts still have skin on them, pour them onto a tea towel (dish towel) while they are still hot, gather the corners together, and roll them around inside the towel to loosen the skins. Then shake the nuts out of the towel to separate them from the skin.

To make a caramel, add the sugar to a saucepan over low heat to gently melt the sugar. Continue to cook until the caramel goes a deep brown, then add the warm hazelnuts, stir until they are coated and then tip them onto a tray to cool slightly.

While the hazelnut caramel is still warm, transfer it to a food processor and blend until very smooth. Weigh 100 g (3½ oz) of the caramel and mix it with the dulce de leche. Spread an even layer of the mixture over the base of the pastry shell. →

Profiteroles

Preheat the oven to 180°C (360°F).

Place the butter, sugar, milk, water and salt in a saucepan and bring to a simmer over medium heat. Once the butter has melted and the mixture has reached a simmer, reduce the heat to low and stir in the flour with a maryse spatula on a low heat. Continue to cook this mixture until a thin film starts to coat the base of the saucepan and the pastry has formed a large lump or ball around your spatula.

Remove the pastry mixture from the saucepan and place into a stand mixer fitted with a paddle attachment. Mix the pastry on low heat to start cooling it down. Once it has come down to 50°C (120°F) add the egg a little at a time until the pastry forms a short 'V' when the paddle is removed from the mix (you may not need the whole amount of egg). Once this has all come together, place the pastry into a piping (pastry) bag with a 10 mm (½ in) piping nozzle attached. Pipe 4 cm (1½ in)-wide domes onto a baking tray (sheet) lined with baking paper. If you have a silicone dome mould with this dimension, a really good way to get a consistent size is to pipe your mix into these moulds, flatten the bases with a palette knife, freeze them, then thaw them on trays once demoulded.

Bake the profiteroles for 25 minutes, then allow to cool at room temperature.

Reduce the oven to 125°C (255°F) to preheat for cooking the custard layer.

Vanilla crème pâtissière

To make the crème pâtissière, bring the milk, half the sugar and vanilla to a boil in a small saucepan over medium heat. Meanwhile, whisk the egg yolks with the rest of the sugar and the cornflour in a bowl. Once the milk has reached a boil, add a small amount to the eggs and whisk to combine. Return this mix to the saucepan and whisk vigorously over a medium heat. Continue to mix until it returns to a boil, then add the butter, a little at a time. Remove the mixture from the heat and give it a quick blend with a hand-held blender. Transfer to a container and place a piece of plastic wrap directly onto the surface of the crème pâtissière to prevent a skin forming.

Once the crème pâtissière has cooled, remove the plastic wrap cover and give it a whisk to break up any lumps. Place roughly 300 g (10½ oz) inside a piping bag to fill the profiteroles, and set the remainder aside.

Caramel

Place a small saucepan over medium heat. Make a direct caramel by heating a saucepan on the stove and gradually

Vanilla custard

Bring the creams, cream cheese, sugar, vanilla and coffee beans to a simmer in a saucepan, then remove from heat. To temper the egg yolks, add them to a mixing bowl and whisk in a small amount of the hot cream mixture until well incorporated. Add the remaining cream mixture and use a hand-held blender to blend until the mixture is shiny and smooth – to prevent any air from being incorporated into the mix, keep the head of the blender underneath the surface. Strain the mixture into a measuring jug through a fine sieve to use straight away – you want to keep it as warm as possible to ensure the mixture cooks evenly in the oven.

Pour this mixture over the hazelnut caramel layer of the tart and bake until slightly wobbly in the centre, around 30 minutes. Remove from the oven, then allow to cool slightly before placing in the fridge to set.

Crème diplomate

Whip the creams to soft peaks in a stand mixer, then add the reserved crème pâtissière and continue to whip to firm peaks. Once stiff, place the cream in a piping bag fitted with a St Honoré nozzle.

Once the custard is cool, place ten of the profiteroles equidistantly around the edge of the vanilla custard. Pipe the crème diplomate into short peaks in between each profiterole, facing outwards, then pipe a whole ring of peaks on the inside of the profiterole circle, ensuring to keep the angle of the peaks consistent. Pipe a second ring inside the piped circle, then place an eleventh profiterole in the middle of the tart.

Portion the tart into slices with a hot, sharp knife (see page 39).

adding the sugar one layer at a time, allowing each layer to fully melt and start to caramelise before adding the next. Once the sugar has fully dissolved and the caramel is a medium brown colour, remove it from heat and allow to cool slightly – the heat will continue to cook the caramel so be sure not to let it get too dark as the residual temperature will cause it to burn. Once the caramel has cooled and thickened somewhat, dip the tops of the profiteroles in the caramel, and then sit them back on their bases so that each profiterole has a clean cap of caramel on top. If you have a dome mould that the profiteroles will fit into, place each one top-side down into the mould so that the caramel sets into a perfect dome shape – it's not essential, but the visual impact is worth it! Once all of the caramel has set, poke a small hole into the bottom of each profiterole with a paring knife, and then cut a hole in the tip of the piping bag so that it will fit inside. Pipe enough custard to fill the entire profiterole, then sit them base-down on a baking tray (sheet) until you assemble.

Savoury
Tarts

Savoury tarts were not at all part of the business model when we opened our first store, but once we had established ourselves as a pastry cafe in Cremorne, we started looking for new ideas and concepts for the tarts.

Working at Lune Croissanterie, Gareth would see many couples come through the doors, and noticed that one person would go for the decadent and sweet pastries and the other would get a simple ham and cheese croissant because that was the only savoury thing on the menu. Working off the idea of tapping into this market, the first savoury tart – our Cheese and Bacon (page 177) or 'The Boyfriend Tart'– was born.

There's some irony in the naming of these tarts, as you'll see as you go through the recipes. The Cheese and Bacon Tart is much, much more than that, consisting of a leek and maple bacon financier topped with a gruyere cheese custard and chives. The Mushroom and Parmesan Tart (page 183) is more accurately a pickled mushroom and sweet-and-sour onion financier topped with a mushroom and parmesan custard. We even serve this one with a shaved truffle add-on when truffle season rolls around. Making a highly 'refined', restaurant-quality savoury tart that sits on a pastry retail counter is no mean feat, and these tarts are, surprisingly, some of the ones we're most proud of.

Our savoury tarts have (rightly) been accused (applauded?) of being bold in flavour and that's what they are, and, we'll add, unashamedly so. That is to say, these are about flavour and we haven't tried to make these a 'healthy option' – they're big, bold and flavourful and unapologetic about that. Gareth often says when he's not hungry, he's still 'hungry for flavour'. Even as a young child Gareth would be in the kitchen creating meals many children would take years to acquire a taste for. At ten years old he invented what he called 'Slop', essentially chopped tomatoes, crispy bacon, onions and mushrooms, all cooked down in a pan with heaps of Worcestershire sauce, to which, once it collapsed into a heap, he would add chopped up toast like a breakfast panzanella. Of course, he didn't understand the fundamentals of cooking at that point – but he did know that the longer he cooked it the browner it would get and therefore the more delicious.

With such beginnings, the evolution of these savoury tarts is worthy of a novel on its own, but suffice to say the biggest achievement has been working out how to incorporate sweetness e.g. the sweet and sour onion chutney, tomato jams, and sweet corn custards. Sugar is key to the balance of these savoury tarts, as it neutralises the salt and acts as a carrier of the flavour explosions we're chasing.

When baking, you'll find that compared to the sweet versions, the savoury tarts are more complex in their number of steps but generally require a little less precision in the making. That being said, don't be a dingus, and still follow the recipe carefully.

Cheese and Bacon Tart

This tart took longer to get right than any other on the menu. The first versions were way too intense; incorporating all the required, but heavy, elements of a tart and achieving a balance of flavour and a final product that was portionable at room temperature was almost impossibly hard. It needed to be textural, not just a tray bake held together by a 'bunch of knackered eggs' (as Gareth would say). But something that required hours of setting was not going to be feasible in the production kitchen. After many iterations, here is the final recipe – it's so good that it seems unlikely it will ever change again.

1 × baked Shortcrust Pastry shell (page 23)
chives, finely chopped, for garnishing

Leek and bacon cake batter
200 g (7 oz) leek, sliced into 2 mm (1/16 in) rounds
200 g (7 oz) smoked speck,
    cut into 1.5 cm (1/2 in) cubes
30 g (1 oz) maple syrup
30 g (1 oz) soft brown sugar
90 g (3 oz) natural almond meal
35 g (1 1/4 oz) plain (all-purpose) flour
2 1/2 g (0.1 oz) baking powder

5 g (0.2 oz) salt
90 g (3 oz) egg
60 g (2 oz) Brown butter (page 111)
olive oil, for frying

Gruyere custard
110 g (4 oz) gruyere cheese
85 g (3 oz) egg yolk
250 g (9 oz) pouring (whipping) cream
2 g salt

Preheat the oven to 165°C (330°F).

Leek and bacon cake batter
Place a large pot of water on the stove and bring to a boil. Season the water with a good amount of salt, approximately 15 g (1/2 oz) per 1 litre (34 fl oz/4 cups) of water. Blanch the sliced leeks in the salted boiling water for 15 seconds. Drain and refresh in iced water, then squeeze out the water from the leeks – you should have approximately 130 g (4 1/2 oz) of leek left.

Add some olive oil to a frying pan and heat on high until it starts to smoke. Add the speck and cook until evenly caramelised on all sides, then remove from the pan and discard the oil. Place the same pan over medium heat and add the maple syrup and the brown sugar. Bring this to a thick and bubbly caramel then return the drained speck pieces. Cook for one minute or until the edges of the speck start to look a little candied. Drain any excess caramel and set aside.

To make the batter, weigh the dry ingredients in a bowl and stir them together. Add the eggs to the mixing bowl of a stand mixer fitted with a whisk attachment and mix on low speed until combined (or do so by hand).

Melt the brown butter in a saucepan. You want this to be warm enough so that the liquid doesn't cool down too quickly, but cool enough so that it doesn't develop any burnt characteristics. If the butter is too hot, it can also fry the egg mixture as you add it, so a thermometer is useful (we aim for roughly 100°C/210°F).

Once the butter comes up to temperature, slowly pour it into the whisked eggs while mixing (or add little by little if whisking by hand). Ensure that the mixture is well emulsified, as this will ensure that the butter doesn't bleed out later making the cake a greasy texture. Then add in the dry ingredients and mix until well combined, ensuring that there are no lumps suspended throughout the batter. →

Vigorously mix the leek and speck into the cake batter by hand to ensure that the leek has been fully distributed and the speck pieces aren't sticking to one another.

To bake

Pour the batter into the pastry shell. Bake the tart for approximately 18 minutes, or until the crust is an even golden brown and the centre of the tart is firm. Remove from the oven and allow to cool inside the tin. Using the back of a spoon, press down firmly on any areas where the cake has risen unevenly so that the surface is flat.

Gruyere custard

Grate the cheese and mix with the egg yolks in a measuring jug, then set aside. Bring the cream and salt to a boil in a saucepan over medium–high heat, then pour it over the egg and cheese. Using a hand-held blender, blitz the custard until it is smooth and glossy. Pour the custard on top of the cake layer, and bake in the oven for 15 minutes, or until it is set.

To finish

Allow to cool at room temperature, then remove the tart from the tin. Using a hot sharp knife, portion the tart into slices (see page 39). Sprinkle an even layer of the cut chives over the top of the tart.

Corn and Jalapeño Tart

For a long time, the Cheese and Bacon (page 177) and Mushroom and Parmesan tarts (page 183) were the only savoury options on the menu. They had taken so long to develop that they sat there for a few months as we built up the energy to tackle a new one. Eventually the idea came to create something using a corn cake, stemming from our love of tamales. The corn cake didn't quite work, as you'll see from the recipe, which uses almonds as well as corn kernels, but from that came a sweet corn custard, paired with pickled jalapeños and cheese. The mountain of parmesan cheese on top is a nod to Dan Hong's revolutionary grilled corn with parmesan and lime, which we first had at Ms. G's in Sydney way back in 2012. It works perfectly here, too.

1 × baked Shortcrust Pastry shell (page 23)
parmesan for grating
lime, for zesting

60 g (2 oz) Brown butter (page 111)
50 g (1¾ oz) grated parmesan
olive oil

Leek, corn and jalapeño cake batter
200 g (7 oz) leek, sliced into 2 mm (1/16 in) rounds
100 g (3½ oz) corn kernels (fresh or frozen)
7 g (¼ oz) salt
90 g (3 oz) almond meal
20 g (¾ oz) pickled jalapeño slices, chopped
35 g (1¼ oz) plain (all-purpose) flour
2.5 g (0.1 oz) baking powder
90 g (3 oz) egg

Corn custard
40 g (1½ oz) butter
200 g (7 oz) corn kernels (fresh or frozen)
210 g (7½ oz) pouring (whipping) cream
20 g (¾ oz) caster (superfine) sugar
7 g (1/4 oz) salt
80 g (2¾ oz) cream cheese
100 g (3½ oz) egg yolk

Preheat the oven to 165°C (330°F).

Leek, corn and jalapeño cake batter
Place a large pot of water on the stove and bring to a boil. Season the water with a good amount of salt – approximately 15 g (½ oz) per 1 litre (34 fl oz/4 cups) of water. Blanch the sliced leeks in the salted boiling water for 15 seconds, then drain and refresh in iced water. Squeeze out the water from the leeks – you should have approximately 130 g (4½ oz) of leek left.

Add some olive oil to a frying pan and heat until it starts to smoke. Add the corn kernels and 2 g of the salt and cook until they are evenly caramelised on all sides, then remove from the pan, discarding the oil.

To make the batter, weigh the dry ingredients, except the parmesan, in a bowl. Add the eggs to the mixing bowl of a stand mixer fitted with a whisk attachment and mix on low speed until combined (or do so by hand).

Melt the brown butter in a saucepan. You want the butter to be warm enough so that the liquid doesn't cool down too quickly, but cool enough so that it doesn't develop any burnt characteristics. If the butter is too hot, it can also fry the egg mixture as you add it, so a thermometer is useful (we aim for roughly 100°C/210°F). →

Once the butter comes up to temperature, slowly pour it into the whisked eggs while mixing (or add little by little if whisking by hand). Ensure that the mixture is well emulsified, as this will ensure that the butter doesn't bleed out later, giving the cake a greasy texture. Then add in the dry ingredients and mix until well combined, ensuring that there are no lumps suspended throughout the batter. Mix the leek, jalapeño, grated parmesan and corn vigorously into the cake batter to ensure that the leek and the corn pieces are fully distributed.

To bake

Pour the batter into the pastry shell. Bake the tart for approximately 18 minutes, or until the crust is an even golden brown and the centre of the tart is firm. Remove from the oven and allow to cool inside the tin. Using the back of a spoon, press down firmly on any areas where the cake has risen unevenly so that the surface is flat. Set aside while you prepare the custard filling.

Reduce the oven temperate to 120°C (250°F) to preheat for baking the custard layer.

Corn custard

Melt the butter in a medium-sized saucepan until foamy, then add the corn kernels. Cook until they their skins are lightly caramelised, then add the cream. Bring the mixture to the boil, then pour into a blender and blitz on the highest speed for 3 minutes. Pass this mix through a fine sieve to remove any corn husk, then weigh 350 g (12½ oz) in a saucepan and add the sugar, salt and cream cheese. Gently heat the mixture, whisking now and then to ensure the cream cheese doesn't catch on the bottom of the pan. Weigh the eggs in a measuring jug and pour in the corn mixture after it's reached a boil. Blend the mixture with a hand-held blender until smooth and glossy, and pour directly over the warm cake layer. Bake for 20 minutes, or until it the custard is firm to the touch.

To finish

Once the custard is cool, remove the tart from the tin and portion into slices with a hot, sharp knife (see page 39). Using a microplane, finish each slice with a generous grating of parmesan, followed by a little lime zest (about a third of a lime's worth).

Mushroom and Parmesan Tart

This tart was quite literally made to be a crowd-pleaser. People kept messaging us on Instagram asking for a vegetarian savoury tart and, after he'd had enough of being bugged, Gareth complied. The result is, in our opinion, the best savoury tart we've ever made. Gareth was very adamant that it would not be a vegetarian version of the Cheese and Bacon Tart (page 177) – he wanted to create something that was delicious in its own right and that just happened to be vegetarian. And in fact, many staunch meat-eaters will attest that this is their favourite of the bunch.

1 × baked Shortcrust Pastry shell (page 23)
parmesan cheese, for grating
chives, finely chopped, for garnishing

Mushroom duxelles
25 g (1 oz) olive oil
400 g (14 oz) button mushrooms, thinly sliced
salt and pepper, to season

Pickled mushrooms
25 g (1 oz) olive oil
200 g (7 oz) button mushrooms,
    sliced 1 cm (½ in thick)
20 g (¾ oz) sherry vinegar
5 g (0.2 oz) caster (superfine) sugar
salt and pepper, to season

Mushroom puree
approx. 200 g (7 oz) cooked button mushrooms,
    leftover from preparing the Mushroom
    duxelles, above
approx. 200 g (7 oz) pouring (whipping) cream,
    see method
salt and pepper, to season

Caramelised onions
150 g (5½ oz) caster (superfine) sugar
5 g (0.2. oz) salt
140 g (5 oz) sherry vinegar
500 g (1 lb 2 oz) onions, sliced

Mushroom cake batter
75 g (2¾ oz) natural almond meal
25 g (1 oz) plain (all-purpose) flour
3 g (0.1 oz) baking powder
4 g (0.14 oz) salt
120 g (4½ oz) egg
85 g (3 oz) Brown butter (page 111)
80 g (2¾ oz) Mushroom duxelles, left
125 g (4½ oz) Pickled mushrooms, left
100 g (3½ oz) Caramelised onions, above

Parmesan custard
95 g (3¼ oz) Parmesan cheese
85 g (3 oz) egg yolk
250 g (9 oz) pouring (whipping) cream
2 g salt
3 g (0.1 oz) sherry vinegar
170 g (6 oz) Mushroom puree, left

Preheat the oven to 165°C (330°F).

Mushroom duxelles
Place a saucepan over high heat and add the olive oil. Once the oil starts to smoke lightly, add the sliced mushrooms, season with salt and pepper and sauté until they are a light golden brown colour. Drain this mixture through a sieve and set aside. Take 80 g (2¾ oz) of the cooked mushrooms and chop them finely with a sharp knife. They should be as small as they can go before they become a puree. Any remaining mushrooms will be used for the mushroom puree (see next page) to avoid waste.

Pickled mushrooms
Add the oil to a pan over high heat and sauté and season the mushrooms as you did for the duxelles. Once they are a light golden brown, turn off the heat and add the sugar and vinegar to deglaze the saucepan. Let this mixture sit for as long as possible to let the vinegar penetrate the mushrooms. →

Mushroom puree
Combine the remaining cooked mushrooms from the duxelles with an equal weight of cream into a saucepan. Bring this mix to a boil and blend until a smooth puree. Season to taste and set aside.

Caramelised onions
Place a frying pan over low heat and add a small amount of the sugar. Allow this to melt and slowly caramelise, then add the remainder. Stir with a wooden spoon until the caramel is an even golden brown. At this point, add the salt and vinegar and increase the heat to bring the mixture to a boil over medium–high heat. Allow this mixture to reduce until the bubbles are thick, then add the onions. Stir with a wooden spoon until the onions start to break down. Continue to simmer this mixture while stirring now and then until the liquid is almost gone and the onions are soft. Pour into a sieve to allow any excess liquid to drain off, then cool in the fridge.

Mushroom cake batter
Weigh the dry ingredients in a bowl and stir them together. Add the eggs to a separate mixing bowl and, using a stand mixer fitted with a whisk attachment, mix until combined on low speed (or do so by hand).

Melt the brown butter in a saucepan. You want this to be warm enough so that the liquid doesn't cool down too quickly, but cool enough so that it doesn't develop any burnt characteristics. If the butter is too hot, it can also fry the egg mixture as you add it, so a thermometer is useful (we aim for roughly 100°C/210°F).

Once the butter comes up to temperature, slowly pour it into the whisked eggs while mixing (or add little by little if whisking by hand). Ensure that the mixture is well emulsified, as this will ensure that the butter doesn't bleed out later, giving the cake a greasy texture. Then add in the dry ingredients and mix until well combined, ensuring that there are no lumps suspended throughout the batter. Vigorously mix the duxelles, pickled mushrooms and onions into the cake batter by hand to ensure that the onions and mushrooms have been fully distributed.

To bake
Pour the mushroom cake batter into the pastry shell. Bake the tart for approximately 18 minutes, or until the crust is an even golden brown and the centre of the tart is springy but not too firm. Remove from the oven and allow to cool inside the tin.

Using the back of a spoon, press down firmly on areas where the cake has risen unevenly so that the surface is flat.

Parmesan custard
To make the parmesan custard, grate the cheese and mix with the egg yolks in a jug and set aside. Bring the cream to the boil with the salt, vinegar and mushroom puree then pour this over the egg and cheese. Using a hand-held blender, blitz the custard until it is smooth and glossy. Pour this mixture over the baked cake layer, and bake again in the oven for 15 minutes, or until it is set.

To finish
Allow to cool at room temperature, then remove the tart from the tin and use a hot, sharp knife to portion into slices (see page 39). Using a microplane, grate a liberal coating of parmesan cheese on top of the slices and garnish with a sprinkling of cut chives.

Sweet Potato, Spinach and Goat's Cheese Tart

This is Catherine's favourite of the savoury tarts and although Gareth would never deign to admit this, if you're looking for a 'lighter' option that's a real brunch crowd pleaser, then this is the one. It is essentially a tart-ified form of the done-to-death (but we can see why) Melbourne brunch menu item of some kind of orange root vegetable, goat's cheese and spinach. Whenever it's on the menu, our baby will happily munch away at the excess sweet potato while we get work done at the shop.

1 × baked Shortcrust Pastry shell (page 23)

Caramelised onions
150 g (5½ oz) caster (superfine) sugar
5 g (0.2 oz) salt
140 g (5 oz) sherry vinegar
500 g (1 lb 2 oz) onions, finely sliced

Leek and sweet potato cake batter
350 g (12½ oz) sweet potato
200 g (7 oz) leek, sliced into 2 mm (1/16 in) rounds
65 g (2¼ oz) natural almond meal
15 g (1/2 oz) plain (all-purpose) flour
2.5 g (0.1 oz) baking powder
3 g (0.1 oz) salt
105 g (3½ oz) egg
75 g (2¾ oz) Brown butter (page 111)
olive oil
salt, to season

Dukkah crumbs
45 g (1½ oz) panko breadcrumbs
20 g (¾ oz) chopped roasted almonds
40 g (1½ oz) dukkah
1 g salt
vegetable oil, for toasting

Spinach and shallot puree
100 g (3½ oz) shallots, sliced thinly
80 g (2¾ oz) vegetable oil
130 g (4½ oz) spinach leaves
100 g (3½ oz) pouring (whipping) cream

Goat's cheese custard
140 g (5 oz) goat's cheese
130 g (4½ oz) Spinach and shallot puree, see above
150 g (5½ oz) pouring (whipping) cream
4 g (0.14 oz) salt
100 g (3½ oz) egg yolk

Preheat the oven to 165°C (330°F).

Caramelised onions
Place a frying pan over low heat and add a small amount of the sugar. Allow this to melt and slowly caramelise, repeat the process with the remainder. Stir with a wooden spoon until the caramel is an even golden brown. At this point, add the salt and vinegar, and bring to a boil over medium–high heat. Allow this mixture to reduce until the bubbles are thick, then add the onions. Stir with a wooden spoon until the onions start to break down. Continue to simmer this mixture, while stirring, until the liquid is almost gone and the onions are soft. Drain off any excess liquid then cool in the fridge.

Leek and sweet potato cake batter
Peel and cut the sweet potato into batons approx. 2 cm (¾ in) thick and 7 cm (2¾ in) long. Toss the sweet potato in a little olive oil and salt, then roast on a tray lined with baking paper for 20 minutes, or until soft. Once cooked, remove from the oven and allow to cool in the fridge until you are ready to assemble the tart.

Place a large pot of water on the stove and bring to a boil. Season the water with a good amount of salt – approximately 15 g (½ oz) per litre (34 fl oz/4 cups) of water. →

Blanch the leek in the salted boiling water for 15 seconds, then drain and refresh in iced water. Squeeze out the water from the leeks – you should have approximately 130 g (4½ oz) of leek left.

To make the batter, first weigh out the dry ingredients in a bowl and stir them together. Add the eggs to a mixing bowl and, using a stand mixer fitted with a whisk attachment, mix until combined on low speed (or do so by hand).

Melt the brown butter in a saucepan. You want this to be warm enough so that the liquid doesn't cool down too quickly, but cool enough so that it doesn't develop any burnt characteristics. If the butter is too hot, it can also fry the egg mixture as you add it, so a thermometer is useful (we aim for roughly 100°C/210°F).

Once the butter comes up to temperature, slowly pour it into the whisked eggs while mixing (or add little by little if whisking by hand). Ensure that the mixture is well emulsified, as this will ensure that the butter doesn't bleed out later, giving the cake a greasy texture. Then add in the dry ingredients and mix until well combined, ensuring that there are no lumps suspended throughout the batter. Vigorously mix the leek into the cake batter by hand to ensure it has been fully distributed.

To assemble and bake
Spread the cake batter into the pastry shell. Take the roasted sweet potato pieces and place into the cake batter in three concentric circles. Use a palette knife to smooth out the cake so that the sweet potato pieces are flush with the level of the cake.

Bake the tart for approximately 18 minutes, or until the crust is an even golden brown and the centre of the tart is firm. Remove from the oven and allow to cool inside the tin. Using the back of a spoon, press down firmly on any areas where the cake has risen unevenly so that the surface is flat.

Spread 150 g (5½ oz) of caramelised onions on top of the cake layer and set aside.

Dukkah crumbs
Heat a small amount of vegetable oil in a small pan and add the panko breadcrumbs. Stir gently to ensure they cook evenly and drain through a sieve once they start to turn a light golden brown – they will continue to colour, so be sure not to take it too far. Mix the fried breadcrumbs with the chopped almonds, dukkah and salt.

Spinach and shallot puree
Add the shallots to a frying pan and cover with the vegetable oil. Bring to a simmer over medium heat, then lower the heat so that the onions can confit gently until they are slightly golden brown in colour. Turn off the heat and allow the shallots to cool in the pan. Bring a large pot of salted water to the boil and blanch the spinach for 1 minute. Drain the spinach and refresh in iced water to keep the colour vibrant. Once refreshed, squeeze out the water from the spinach and add to a saucepan along with the drained shallots. Stir to combine over medium–high heat. Once cooled slightly, add to a blender and blend for 2 minutes, or until smooth. Reserve the puree in the fridge until needed.

Goat's cheese custard
Bring the cheese, spinach and shallot puree, cream and salt to a simmer in a saucepan. Meanwhile, add the egg yolks to a tall measuring jug. Once the mixture has come to a simmer, pour it into the jug with the eggs and using a hand-held blender, blitz the custard until it is smooth and glossy. Pour this mixture over of the jam layer in the pastry shell and bake the tart for 15 minutes, or until the custard is set.

To finish
Allow to cool at room temperature, then remove from the tart from the tin and portion into slices with a hot, sharp knife (see page 39). Dust each slice with an even sprinkling of the dukkah crumb.

Smoked Potato and Chorizo Tart

This tart was meant to be a Spanish-inspired version of the Cheese and Bacon Tart. We had been developing it alongside a tomato tart that we never did get right, but the tomato jam we created during testing was amazing, so eventually the two ideas were combined – and this is the delicious result. It may seem against your better judgement to blend potatoes into a puree, however, once baked with the egg and cream, this process helps the potato set for clean portioning. Not to mention the ever-so-smooth potato custard texture, which speaks for itself.

1 × baked Shortcrust Pastry shell (page 23)

Potato puree
500 g (1 lb 2 oz) royal blue potatoes
approx. 200 g (7 oz) pouring (whipping) cream

Parsley crumbs
vegetable oil, for frying
70 g (2½ oz) panko breadcrumbs
5 g (0.2 oz) flat leaf parsley
1 g salt

Tomato jam
50 g (1¾ oz) caster (superfine) sugar
50 g (1¾ oz) sherry vinegar
250 g (9 oz) white onions, finely diced
3 g (0.1 oz) salt
175 g (6 oz) canned crushed tomatoes
2 g dried oregano

Leek and chorizo cake batter
200 g (7 oz) leek, sliced into 2 mm (1/16 in) rounds
200 g (7 oz) chorizo, cut into approx.
    1.5 cm (½ in) rounds
90 g (3 oz) natural almond meal
35 g (1¼ oz) plain (all-purpose) flour
2.5 g (0.1 oz) baking powder
5 g (0.2 oz) salt
90 g (3 oz) egg
60 g (2 oz) Brown butter (page 111)
Olive oil, for frying

Smoked potato custard
270 g (9½ oz) Potato puree, left
135 g (5 oz) pouring (whipping) cream
2 g smoke powder
4 g (0.14 oz) salt
90 g (3 oz) egg yolk

Preheat the oven to 180°C (360°F).

Potato puree
To make the potato puree, place the potatoes, whole and unpeeled, straight on a rack in the oven and bake for 1 hour. Once the potatoes can be stabbed with a paring knife with no resistance, remove from the oven and allow to cool before peeling. Weigh the cooked potatoes and place in a saucepan with an equal amount of cream and bring to a simmer. Remove the saucepan from the heat and break up the potatoes with a whisk. Then, blend until smooth using a hand-held blender. Pass the puree through a fine sieve to remove any rogue lumps, then set aside.

Parsley crumbs
Heat a small pan of vegetable oil and add the panko breadcrumbs. Stir gently to ensure the breadcrumbs cook evenly and start to turn a light golden brown – they will continue to colour, so be sure not to take it too far. Strain through a sieve, reserving the oil. Place the fried breadcrumbs on paper towel to drain. →

Using the reserved oil, fry the picked parsley leaves until the oil stops bubbling and the parsley leaves are opaque but not turning brown. Place the fried parsley on paper towel to drain. Once cool, crush the parsley leaves slightly and mix together with the salt and breadcrumbs.

Tomato jam

Heat a medium saucepan on the stove, add the caster sugar and stir with a wooden spoon to ensure it is cooking to an even golden-brown caramel. Add the sherry vinegar and bring to a boil. Then, stir in the onions and the salt and cook on a low heat until the onions start to collapse and become transparent and brown. Once the liquid has all but evaporated, add the crushed tomatoes and oregano and cook until the mixture thickens. Reduce the jam until it becomes a thick paste, then decant into a container to cool.

Leek and chorizo cake batter

Place a large pot of water on the stove and bring to a boil. Season the water with a good amount of salt – approximately 15 g (½ oz) per 1 litre (34 fl oz) of water. Blanch the leek in the salted boiling water for 15 seconds, then drain and refresh in iced water. Squeeze out the water from the leeks – you should have approximately 130 g (4½ oz) of leek left.

Add a little olive oil to a frying pan and heat over high heat it until it starts to smoke. Add the chorizo pieces and cook until they are evenly caramelised on all sides, then remove from the pan and discard the oil.

Weigh the dry ingredients in a bowl. Add the eggs to a mixing bowl and, using a stand mixer fitted with a whisk attachment, mix until combined on low speed (or do so by hand).

Melt the brown butter in a saucepan. You want this to be warm enough so that the liquid doesn't cool down too quickly, but cool enough so that it doesn't develop any burnt characteristics. If the butter is too hot, it can also fry the egg mixture as you add it, so a thermometer is useful (we aim for roughly 100°C/210°F).

Once the butter comes up to temperature, slowly pour it into the whisked eggs while mixing (or add little by little if whisking by hand). Ensure that the mixture is well emulsified, as this will ensure that the butter doesn't bleed out later, giving the cake a greasy texture. Then add in the dry ingredients and mix until well combined, ensuring that there are no lumps suspended throughout the batter. Mix the leek and chorizo vigorously into the cake batter to ensure that the leek and the chorizo pieces are fully distributed.

To bake

Pour the batter into the pastry shell. Bake the tart for approximately 18 minutes, or until the crust is an even golden brown and the centre of the tart is firm. Remove from the oven and allow to cool inside the tin.

Using the back of a spoon, press down firmly on any areas where the cake has risen unevenly so that the surface is flat. Spread 150 g (5½ oz) of tomato jam on top of the cake and set aside while you make the custard filling.

Smoked potato custard

Bring the potato puree, cream, smoke powder and salt to the boil in a saucepan. Meanwhile, add the egg yolks to a tall measuring jug. Once the cream mixture has reached a boil, pour it over the egg yolks and blend with a hand-held blender until smooth and glossy. Pour this mixture on top of the jam layer and bake for 15 minutes, or until the custard is set.

To finish

Allow to cool at room temperature, then remove from the tin. Portion the tart into slices using a hot, sharp knife (see page 39) and sprinkle an even layer of the parsley crumbs onto each slice.

Potato and Raclette Tart

Inspired by a Swiss raclette, this is the first tart we made in which the bottom layer of the tart isn't actually cooked inside the pastry shell. That may seem like we're just making any old thing, putting it in a pastry shell and calling it a tart, and well, in this case, we are. There's always an exception to the rule! The potatoes here are cooked lyonnaise style then placed into the blind-baked pastry shell after the fact. We do this process the day before, so the next day you can place the potatoes straight inside the pastry shell and bake the custard on top. This tart would make an epic addition to a hearty winter dinner spread. Or, if you don't want to make a tart but for some reason are looking at a tart cookbook for inspiration (strange but could happen), you can also just use the recipe for potatoes lyonnaise. You will not be disappointed.

---

1 × baked Shortcrust Pastry shell (page 23)

Caramelised onions
150 g (5½ oz) caster (superfine) sugar
500 g (1 lb 2 oz) onions, finely sliced
5 g (0.2 oz) salt
140 g (5 oz) sherry vinegar

Potatoes lyonnaise
260 g (9 oz) royal blue potatoes, or similar
3 g (0.1 oz) rosemary sprigs, chopped
5 g (0.2 oz) thyme leaves
2 g salt
1 g pepper

120 g (4½ oz) Caramelised onions, above
30 g (1 oz) olive oil

Potato crumbs
250 g (9 oz) frozen french fries
vegetable oil, for frying
10 g (¼ oz) chives, finely chopped

Raclette custard
110 g (4 oz) smoked raclette cheese
85 g (3 oz) egg yolk
250 g (9 oz) pouring (whipping) cream
2 g salt

Preheat the oven to 180°C (360°F).

Caramelised onions
Place a frying pan over low heat and add a small amount of the sugar. Allow this to melt and slowly caramelise, then repeat the process with the remainder. Stir with a wooden spoon until the caramel is an even golden brown. At this point, add the salt and vinegar, then increase the heat to high to bring to a boil. Allow this mixture to reduce until the bubbles are thick, then reduce the heat to medium and add the onions. Stir with a wooden spoon until the onions start to break down. Continue to simmer this mixture, while stirring, until the liquid is almost gone and the onions are soft. Pour into a sieve to allow any excess liquid to drain off, then cool in the fridge.

Potatoes lyonnaise
Line an empty tart tin with a large piece of aluminium foil that can hang over the edges – this will be folded over the top later. Cut a piece of baking paper to size so that it will fit inside the bottom of the tart tin and place it inside the foil layer. Trim the sides of the potatoes if necessary, so that they can fit on a mandolin, then slice them to roughly 1–2 mm (1/32–1/16 in) thin. Combine the rosemary, thyme, salt and pepper in a bowl and mix together.

Next, place a slightly overlapping layer of potatoes on the bottom of the tin, roughly 240 g (8½ oz), reinforcing the edges to ensure an even and level layer. Spread 100 g (3½ oz) of the caramelised onions on top of the potatoes and follow with a drizzle of olive oil. →

Sprinkle a good amount of the herby salt mix over the top and repeat this process until you have run out of potatoes, making sure to finish with a complete layer of potato, you should have approximately two layers of caramelised onion. Place a piece of baking paper on the surface of the potatoes, then gently fold over the overhanging aluminium foil to ensure that the potato is covered without disrupting the shape too much. Bake for 60 minutes.

Once a sharp knife can pierce the potatoes easily, remove from the oven and allow to cool at room temperature. Once the potato cool enough to handle, place a plate (or something flat and the same size as the tart tin) on top and weigh it down with something large and heavy. Leave overnight in the fridge to compress the layers.

The next day, remove the weight and the foil, then peel off the baking paper. Place the potato onto a tray, then use a plate to flip the potato upside down and remove it from the tin. Peel off the baking paper and use some paper towel to dab off any excess oil or moisture. Remove any loose bits of potato or onion. Flip upside down a second time, then slide the potato into the baked pastry shell.

Potato crumbs
Take the frozen French fries and blitz them quickly in a food processor until they form a fine crumb. Fill a large frying pan a quarter full of vegetable oil and heat to 180°C (355°F). Be sure to leave lots of room in the pot for the oil to bubble up as you add the potato. Drop the potato crumbs into the hot oil and whisk them as they cook to prevent them from sticking together. Once they are an even golden-brown colour and the oil is bubbling less, pour the oil and fried potato through a sieve to drain the oil. Let it sit for a few seconds then pour the fried potato crumble onto a tray or a plate lined with absorbent paper towel. Sprinkle on some salt, then set aside.

Raclette custard
Reduce the oven to 125°C (255°F). Place the tart in the oven for 10 minutes or so to reheat the potato base. This will allow the heat to properly conduct through the bottom of the tart and allow the custard to cook evenly.

Next, grate the cheese and mix with the egg yolks in a tall measuring jug and set aside. Bring the cream and salt to the boil in a saucepan, then pour it over the egg and cheese. Using a hand-held blender, blitz the custard until smooth and glossy. Pour this mixture on top of the potato layer, and bake in the oven for 15 minutes, or until the custard set. Allow to cool at room temperature.

To finish
Once cool, remove the tart from the tin and portion into slices with a hot, sharp knife (see page 39). Mix 90 g (3 oz) of the potato crumbs with 10 g (¼ oz) of chopped chives, then spread an even layer of the mixture over the slices.

The Trim

Quick Troubleshooting Guide

Let us assure you there are going to be hiccups. Pastry cracks, it's prone to shrinkage and it's difficult to know when a custard is baked perfectly.

Here are some of the issues that we are asked about (and encounter ourselves) often. While the techniques and explanations in this book will aim to foolproof your tart baking, please don't be discouraged if this is your most referenced section of the book! Maybe you can't polish a turd but you sure can polish a tart.

Common Issues

Blonde pastry

Blonde pastry is a very sensitive subject. Some people love the almost doughy texture of a meat pie crust that could have used an extra 10 minutes in the oven. However, when making tarts that may need to be baked up to three times, this texture usually isn't achievable. Once you start introducing fillings that need their own baking, the cooking of the crust is essentially put on hold until the filling has done its thing.

So to avoid undercooking pastry like this, people are tempted on occasion to check the pastry during blind baking and will sometimes even remove the blind baking weights just to finish it off. Shortcrust pastry's inclination to shrink makes baking without weights, regardless of doneness, a bad idea. So, keep the weights inside the shell and continue to cook until it is an even colour throughout – even if it means reducing the oven temperature slightly.

Cracks

Cracking is something that will always be a looming threat to the tart maker. Pastry that hasn't been completely mixed together will be prone to cracking as there aren't any bonds to hold it together. With pastry made the way that we do it, shrinkage is a very real and ever present problem. And when the pastry wants to retract, it will always find the path of least resistance, which usually means cracking.

The best way to resolve this is to reinforce any weaker areas, whether it be a crease, a hole, an unmixed section of pastry, or an area where the pastry has dried out. Use a small piece of scrap pastry from the trimmed edges and press into the areas that look as though they might open up. Once they are baked, you can use a microplane to shave down any overhanging bits that have been used to patch a hole. No one will ever know!

Pastry glue

Pastry glue (see page 109) was a little trick that I learnt from Heston Blumenthal. He would blend the trim from the edges of the pastry with a little egg and a splash of water to create a thick paste that could be used to repair any cracks in the shell. We've adopted this technique as protection or a 'bonding' element for tarts such as the Honey and Almond Shortbread Tart (also page 109) where the shortbread would normally not fuse to the pastry. This is also a great way to repair smaller cracks that could potentially leak custard or other fillings. We always make up a small batch of this every couple of days for handyman jobs.

Puffing

Puffing will only happen to the pastry in two instances: if the dough is overworked and therefore air is introduced into the dough, or if the weights used to blind bake aren't snug enough and there is space between the pastry and the lining. In the case of the former, you would really need to over-work the pastry rather significantly to establish a gluten network capable of holding air pockets, similar to bread. As for not having enough rice (or any other weight) to weigh down the pastry as it cooks, little bubbles can start to appear on areas of the pastry – and although delicious in the ways of texture, these can disrupt the structural integrity of the tart and aesthetic.

Brûlée-ing

People always argue which sugar is the best for brûlée. We use caster (superfine) sugar because the finer sugar means that it melts faster. The faster the sugar melts, the more control you have over how it caramelises, instead of waiting extra time for the larger crystals of a granulated sugar to become fluid and therefore begin colouring before its fully liquid. It's just science really.

A blowtorch has always been considered a must-have for this technique. When I was a very green apprentice making brûlées we once ran out of gas in the kitchen, which would usually spell disaster for this technique. But needs must and it turns out that heating up a large kitchen spoon on the gas burner and using the scalding metal to caramelise the sugar is a very resourceful way to circumvent this problem if you don't have a blow torch.

Perfect custards

Perfecting baked custards is one of hardest things to teach. In so many recipes, times and temperature will always be a great measuring stick to abide by. But the baked custard is one that requires understanding and observation – it's something that takes a bit of time to get a handle on. There are warning signs, of course, but knowing the difference between a 'wobble', a 'jiggle' and a 'shiver' is key to getting the set on those custards just right.

Low cooking temperatures are very important, but having the temperature of the custard high enough before baking is critical. Baking from a cold custard mixture means that the outside areas of the custard will begin cooking before the centre – eggy custard around the edges of your tart is a common sign of this. Keeping your custard mixture warm once you have assembled it will get you the quick, even cook you desire.

From there, residual heat is king. The setting point of egg is around 84°C (183°F), so getting the centre of the custard to that temperature is the goal. An oven set to 125°C (255°F), the temperate we bake custards at, can have hot spots, and fans can push heat around unevenly, so things are not always going to happen like in the movies. Keep an eye on how the custard is baking throughout the process by giving the shelf or tin a little tap to see how the mixture is moving. If it's almost at the point that you are after (we're usually looking for a slight wobble in the centre), sometimes opening the door and allowing the tart to sit in that warm environment for a few minutes will just tide it over without putting extra heat into parts of the custard that are already at the optimum temperature.

Index

Acknowledgements

To Otis, you will never fully understand the impact that you had on the making of this book – the joy of watching you grow and become the bubbly and joyful boy you are at the time of writing has inspired me to be someone that one day you'll look up to.

To my parents, Maureen and Rob, the endless support and encouragement you've provided my entire life and career has been paramount to where I am today. And to Dom, James, Liam, Caitlin and Sophia, the love and tight knit family network we have built together over the last 30-odd years has only empowered me to out-do all you battlers and finally be the favourite child.

For the Tarts Anon family, this one's for you. I have been remarkably lucky to be able to call all of you my friends and colleagues, particularly the ones who have been along for the ride and then some. Kitty, GG, Alice, Anna, Nina and Marc, your comradery and loyalty has been so important to how our business has evolved over the years, and to have been on this journey with you (in three different establishments for some of you), has truly been the maker of the chef I am today – and all of our achievements are testament to this.

To Xavier, you are as much a part of Tarts Anon as anyone. Your dedication to the cause as well as your own personal development has been exemplary. The man you have become has exhibited the personal and professional growth that you have undergone – and the application of this to your work and how you have developed and nurtured your team is something I am forever grateful for.

To my friend and oftentimes professional therapist Melissa Leong – thank you so much for your support and of course your beautiful words. Getting to know you has coincided with some of the most pivotal moments of my career, and I am very grateful to have shared these with you.

To Amaury, Phil and Ashley I'd like to say thank you for all of the help and kindness you have shown in assisting in promoting this book.

Catherine and I would like to thank everyone who has been involved in bringing this book together. Claire Orrell, Armelle Habib and Lee Blaylock – the simplistic elegance that this book has in droves is all thanks to the creative brilliance and insightful harmony that we shared through the design and shooting of these pages. Thank you.

To the Hardie Grant team, Michael Harry, Simon Davis, Ruby Goss, Elena Callcott and Kristin Thomas. Working with you, alongside Nola James and Helena Holmgren, has been an absolute pleasure and has made making this book not only a smooth and seamless process, but a joyous and thrilling ride. Thank you for your meticulous and persistent emails and insufferable attention to detail. It was totally worth it.

To all our friends, family and former colleagues who have been so instrumental in making me feel like what I was getting up to wasn't a waste of time and that it would at some point pay off. I never thought I'd need to look back and see what people's support would mean to me. Huge thanks.

Grant, Katrina and all the Pier OGs, Kim, Analiese, Harry, the Oud Sluis team, DBH Alumni (London and Melbourne), the Dawgs, Bowral crew, DM Homies, Leon and Nathan, collecting all of you as friends and support over the years is a pretty good indication of how this isn't a flop. Cheers.

Finally, to the original Tarts Anon fans (aka tart-holes), who lined up outside our Richmond apartment during COVID and showed an unfathomable amount of support and enthusiasm for what we were doing. Thank you to Sabrina Gough, Tyrone Andres, Mel, Shawn and Cherie, Holly Hansen, Alex Clark, and so, so many more. You guys are part of our story and we are forever grateful.

Final Vows

We've been together for ten years, own a house, have a baby, share a troubled dog and co-own a business but never got married. Maybe one day, but for now we thought it would be cute to write some vows to each other for the end of the book that we can read from each other once it's published.

CW: Gareth, wow! We wrote a cookbook and I presume both of us are still alive to tell the tale. What an incredible journey we've been on together. I always joke that, shacked up together in lockdown, you begrudgingly humoured me by going along with my plan to make some extra cash on the weekend. And, while it's true you never would have started this business without me (don't forget it!) there's no denying that while anyone could have had my idea, there's only one person on this earth who could have executed it the way you have. Tarts Anon has succeeded beyond even my wildest imaginings, and there's no way that this isn't a testament to your dedication to your craft, eye for detail and your decision, every day, to settle for nothing less than perfection. While at times I'll admit this has frustrated me, the level at which you operate our business is incredible and I am certain this is the foundation that will continue to see its success. Anything I have contributed is superfluous to your undeniable talent, passion and hard work that has ensured the success of this business. So, to my partner in business and also in life, you are equal parts passionate, funny and sweet and I wouldn't have the Gareth recipe any other way. Hiring you as my head pastry chef was one of the best decisions I've ever made. I love you.

GW: Catherine, thank you for everything you have contributed to the Tarts Anon journey. From sitting on the living room floor scrolling through DMs, to pulling long shifts on the counter at our first store while pregnant, taking sole responsibility of HR, Accounts, FOH operations, Social Media, Marketing, PR and everything in between – you have really proved your throwaway line of 'Gareth bakes the tarts, Cat does the everything else' to be more correct than you ever would have predicted. On top of this, you have taken all of this on while being pregnant, and then while taking care of our amazing and outrageously restless son, Otis, from infancy, right up to the talkative, happy, bottomless pit of energy that he is today. You are a remarkably intelligent, caring, supportive and dynamic woman and I'm so proud and grateful to have been able to share this journey, and this wonderful chronicling of our great achievement, with you.

Published in 2024 by Hardie Grant Books,
an imprint of Hardie Grant Publishing

Hardie Grant Books (Melbourne)
Wurundjeri Country
Building 1, 658 Church Street
Richmond, Victoria 3121

Hardie Grant North America
2912 Telegraph Ave
Berkeley, California 94705

hardiegrant.com/books

Hardie Grant acknowledges the Traditional
Owners of the Country on which we work, the
Wurundjeri People of the Kulin Nation and
the Gadigal People of the Eora Nation, and
recognises their continuing connection to the
land, waters and culture. We pay our respects
to their Elders past and present.

A catalogue record for this
book is available from the
National Library of Australia

Tarts Anon
ISBN 978 1 74379 931 4
ISBN 978 1 76144 071 7 (ebook)

10 9 8 7 6 5 4 3 2 1

Publishers: Michael Harry, Simon Davis
Project Editor: Elena Callcott
Editor: Ruby Goss
Design Manager: Kristin Thomas
Designer: Claire Orrell
Photographer: Armelle Habib
Stylist: Lee Blaylock
Head of Production: Todd Rechner
Production Controller: Jessica Harvie

Colour reproduction by
Splitting Image Colour Studio

Printed in China by
Leo Paper Products LTD.

The paper this book is printed on is from
FSC®-certified forests and other sources.
FSC® promote s environmentally responsible,
socially beneficial and economically viable
management of the world's forests.